# KATE BUTTERS'
# SCRAPBOOK

## EXTRAORDINA
## EXTRAORDIN
## EXTRAORDINAI

GW00724702

### Edited by C. Michael Collins

The King's Head

KATE BUTTERS' SCRAPBOOK
EXTRAORDINARY PLACE
EXTRAORDINARY TIME
EXTRAORDINARY PERSON

First Published privately as Kate Butters' Scrapbook in 2018
by C Michael Collins,
for the sole use of Peter and Sybil King

This Edition first published in Great Britain in 2019
by CZ Design & Print

ISBN: 978-1-9162073-0-1

A catalogue copy of this book is available from the British Library.

Printed and bound by CZ Design & Print
Visit www.czdesignandprint.co.uk for any further information.

Cover design created and made available by Lisa Zador
(c) 2012 Lisa Zador
www.curiousprintandpattern.com

"The King's Head" clay panel on the previous page was made by Kate
to recognise that her house had once been The King's Head Inn

# CONTENTS

4   Time Line
5   Gooby Family Tree
7   Introduction
9   My Mother's Early Days
13  Memories of a "Railway Child"
19  Elsenham Parochial School
23  Sweets and Treats
28  Games of My Childhood
33  Secondary Education
34  Centenary of Thaxted School 1880 - 1980
36  The Dunmow Fellowship
39  Changes and Highlights in Thaxted School from 1925
43  1934 - Milk was Issued to Children, ⅓pt for ½d
46  War Memories
48  Memories of a Teacher in Thaxted School During World War
    II - The Evacuees
52  School Days During World War II
55  Tribute by Bruce Munro
58  Thaxted Discovers America 1943
64  Essex Education Committee Letters
66  A Collection of Kind Words
67  From a tribute given by Sybil Collings - 17th March 2003
68  Some Memories of Being Musician to the Thaxted Morris Men
73  Music in my Life
76  "Doing the Flowers" in Church
82  Part of the Story of Church House
88  The Garden at Church House, Thaxted
92  Letters from America
95  From a tribute given by Sybil Collings - 17th March 2003
96  Kate the Film Star
97  Kate makes British Pathe News
98  Lament for the Departed

# KATE BUTTERS' TIME LINE

| | |
|---|---|
| 1867 | Kate's Mother born |
| 1899 | Kate born in Isleham Fen |
| 1900 | Family moves to Elsenham |
| 1904 | Starts at Elsenham Village School |
| 1905 | Moves from "Babies" class to "First" class |
| 1910 | Thaxted Light Railway construction starts |
| 1912 | Starts at Herts & Essex High School |
| 1917 | Starts at Avery Hill Teacher Training College |
| 1919 | Starts at Upshire Primary School, Waltham Abbey |
| 1920 | Kate's father dies – all leave the Railway |
| 1921 | Starts at Thaxted County Primary School (TCPS) |
| 1924 | Dunmow Fellowship founded |
| 1925 | Mr Bunting retires – Mr Jenner became Head of TCPS |
| 1927 | School remodelled |
| 1929 | First NE Essex Sports held |
| 1932 | Kate and Arthur purchased Church House |
| 1934 | Milk first issued at cost of 1/2d for 1/3 pint |
| 1935 | Thaxted Pageant |
| 1937 | Electricity comes to TCPS |
| 1942 | First American seen in Thaxted |
| 1946 | School Milk now free |
| 1947 | Start of American connections |
| 1949 | Mr Jenner retires, Mr Bennett acting Head |
| 1950 | Mr Westcott became Head – Seniors went to S.Walden |
| 1959 | Kate retires |
| 2003 | Kate dies, aged 103 |

# GOOBY FAMILY TREE

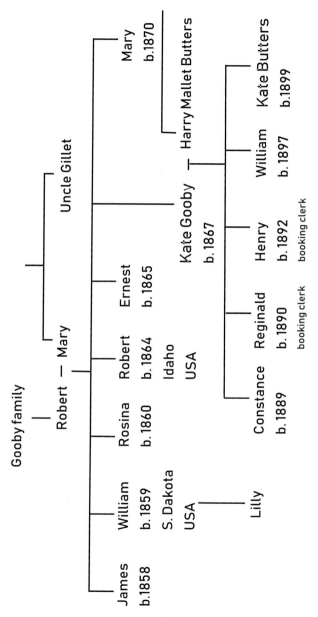

Gooby family

Robert — Mary

Uncle Gillet

James
b.1858

William
b.1859
S. Dakota
USA

Lilly

Rosina
b.1860

Robert
b.1864
Idaho
USA

Ernest
b.1865

Mary
b.1870

Kate Gooby
b.1867

Harry Mallet Butters

Constance
b.1889

Reginald
b.1890
booking clerk

Henry
b.1892
booking clerk

William
b.1897

Kate Butters
b.1899

Information drawn from 1871 and 1901 census

One day I saw Kate standing looking across the road,
seemingly at nothing.
"What are you looking at? I asked.
"I'm looking at the old tree that used to be there."
There was wisdom.

# KATE BUTTERS' SCRAPBOOK

*A woman who did not seek material wealth, but was lively, creative, fulfilled and at peace with herself. She influenced all those with whom she came into contact.*

## INTRODUCTION

In a house in Thaxted, not far from the Parish Church, resides a somewhat ordinary looking scrapbook. Open it up and you discover a wealth of writings and some photos that transport you back through time. This resource was recognised as being too important to remain unseen by more than a few, but its delicate physical nature also demanded its careful handling. This book sets out to be the answer to that conundrum.

I have not written a biography of Kate. That is for someone else to do. This book is also not a facsimile of the scrapbook. But what I have done is gathered Kate's writings, just as she wrote them, and assembled them into what I hope is a logical, readable form. I felt it was important to leave the text exactly as she wrote it, which was just as she spoke, While working on this project, other pieces of Kate's writings came my way, so also had to be included. The pieces were written over many years, so inevitably some anecdotes are found in more than one story.

The writings are interspersed with biographical information and photographs. Then it is spiced up with some of the recollections of those who knew Kate. These are printed in italics.

Thank you Peter and Sybil King for showing me Kate's Scrapbook and giving me the opportunity to work with it: plus many Kate stories.

Thank you to all those who have supported the idea and provided me with their memories and photographs. Particularly Sue Bush, Mike Goatcher, Mick Mullis and Bruce Munro.

C. MICHAEL COLLINS - EDITOR

A visitor to Church House remarked to Kate that she had a lovely view from her window.

"It was even better before they built that church."

That was one of her quips.

Another was, "They never asked our permission to build it!"

And there were many other versions of this story!

# MY MOTHER'S EARLY DAYS.

My mother, Kate Gooby, was born in 1867 at the Plough Inn in Littleport in the Isle of Ely. She was the youngest but one of a big family of four sons and three daughters. Her father was a barge owner who kept his boats on the River Ouse, which was just across the road from his house, and was hidden from it by the very steep banks which protected the surrounding flat countryside from floods. These barges were towed by horses which walked along on the high banks and often they had to jump over fences erected at various points. Those horses with rat like tails were reckoned to be the best jumpers. So said my Uncle Ernest. The four sons had to help with the barge work, which meant carrying coal and various goods from the nearby railway dock to outlying farms in the Fens. They would then bring back wheat, barley and oats, or sometimes perhaps potatoes from the farms back to Littleport or beyond. They would go as far afield or I should say "awater" or "ariver" as Cambridge, Kings Lynn, Mildenhall and so on and were often away from home for several weeks at a time. One barge was fitted up with cabins, bunks, cooking stoves and stores, for they had to fend for themselves.

It was a hard life for the boys, but they seemed to thrive on it, and were never too tired to amuse themselves and others with music and, singing. They played concertinas and banjos. William made a banjo when he was 12 years old, and would give impromptu concerts in the barn of the inn. Sometimes they would take a dinghy and go up to the Backs at Cambridge and with their blackened faces, their playing and singing gave great amusement to the students, who no doubt helped to fill their purses.

Later, incidentally, two of them, William and Robert emigrated to America, where they started small farm settlements in South Dakota and Idaho. A third brother James went to South Africa during the Boer War, and settled as a watch-maker and maker of musical instruments. The youngest son Ernest was left to help carry on the lighterman's work on the barges, 'tho he wanted to go out and join his two brothers in The States. He carried on the business for many years until motor power ousted the horse-drawn barges, and the farmers owned lorries for their own cartage. The end of these lovely old tarred lighters was rather heroic, they were filled with concrete and dropped into the great holes made when the river burst its banks and flooded the Fens in 1947.

To go back to the story of my mother, from which I have digressed, she did not live at home long with this happy family, for she was "borrowed" by an aunt and uncle who had a general store and bakery business at Black Horse Drove, a kind of small hamlet about a mile and half from Littleport. They had no children of their own and eventually they adopted my mother when she was 4 yrs old. She went to the little Board School on the drove, and once was kept in for some misdemeanour. She was locked in and forgotten about, so she climbed out through a window. I remember her telling me how she wore pattens over her shoes or boots in the winter as a protection from the mud. If it happened to be a very severe winter the river, which was close by, might get frozen over, and then she could skate on it all the way up to Littleport to visit her Mother and the family. She learned to play the harmonium, probably from her Uncle Gillet who played the clarinet and bass viol, and she often played the hymns in the little chapel on Sundays. One day there was a rather new and difficult tune for one hymn and she was finding it hard to keep in with the singing. But an old man standing near gave her some good advice, "Pucker it in gal, pucker it in," which she proceeded to do and no doubt all was well.

When she was older, she was sent to a school in Ely as a weekly boarder, where she was much ridiculed because of her nightcaps, which her aunt insisted on her wearing to keep the pillow slips clean. When her uncle took her to Ely, this was the procedure: they would walk to the river bank, just at the end of the drove, with the horse, put all in the boat, luggage, little girl and the horse, and cross to the other side of the river, where uncle kept a trap in a shed, and where the road followed the river from Kings Lynn. Then came a six mile drive to Ely and school.

When she left school she helped in the shop, and learned from her aunt, how to cook and keep house, and how to make good bread from her uncle who was a master baker from London. When she was twenty she met a handsome young clerk named Harry Mallet Butters working in the booking office at Littleport railway station. They fell in love, and were shortly married. Her wedding dress was a lovely pale grey stiff silk one, with a boned and fitted bodice, buttoned down the front with many little silver buttons, and complete with a small bustle at the back. The colour, material, and style were chosen "to come in useful", and the skirt no doubt did do so as only the bodice was left. We often used to get it out of its resting place and admire its pretty pleats and buttons. They went to live in Doncaster, and my mother was pleased with the big north-country oven in which to cook her Fen bread, and so began my mother's married life.

---

*My first experience of Kate Butters was when I came to Thaxted as a newly married woman, so I didn't know anyone. I came to work in the bank, Barclays, having been transferred from Dunmow and on my first week on the tills this lady came to the desk with a cheque signed by Arthur Caton. And it was a woman, so I said, "I'm sorry, but I can't cash that cheque as you are obviously not Arthur Caton." You could hear the air being taken out of the room as everyone else behind me realised who she was. She turned and said, "Now look here! Do you know who I am?" I replied "No, but I think I am going to find out!"*

*That is the sort of thing you don't forget.*

# MEMORIES OF A "RAILWAY CHILD"

I was born in the station house at Isleham Fen, a station on a branch line from Cambridge to Mildenhall, so I count myself a "Fen Tiger" like my mother who was from Littleport in the Isle of Ely. When I was six months old my father was promoted to be station master at Elsenham on the main line from London to Cambridge. This was a great change in many ways, many more trains, fast expresses and of course traffic all night. My father spent the first night there, alone, in an empty house with the open bedroom window facing the oncoming traffic and owned to being scared stiff at the noise of the first fiery express that woke him up! However the family moved in and soon settled down to a new and busier life; though it was still country. So we could still have Bess, our donkey, a goat which used to pull my red painted mail-cart, chickens and of course pigs. Before I was old enough to go to the village school, I can remember playing in the garden which overlooked the station forecourt and level crossing with gates linking the roads from Elsenham to Henham. Anyone in a cart on the forecourt wanting to go to Henham had to call out "Gates" for a porter to come and open them. One such farmer who was always in a hurry and also very impatient would shout loudly and angrily for "Gates". One day when he had been shouting and shouting for "Gates", I was heard to say "Take 'em den", quite a good solution from a three-year-old.

Our dining room window looked out on this forecourt, so we had a fine view of all the vehicles which came there, either bringing people for the trains or to meet them coming off.

There were Rogers' buses from Thaxted, dog carts, governess carts, private traps from the nearby villages or the fine carriages of Sir Walter Gilbey from Elsenham Hall. It was great fun to watch all the different passengers and their drivers and to try and guess who they were and what was their business or pleasure. We saw the latest Paris fashions when the fine ladies came to visit at the Hall. These were the days before the motor car, and Sir Walter's horses and carriages were something to see. Sometimes his beautiful racehorses would be brought down to the station from the paddocks all very carefully bandaged and blanketed, to be loaded into horse boxes to go to Newmarket perhaps for the races or to shows. He was a famous breeder of racehorses as well as a businessman in the wine and spirit world.

I will digress here to say how he was interested in my father's effort to make the station platform attractive with shrubs etc. So he had brought over from his chateaux in France lovely pink rose bushes enough to line both platforms in front of the laurels, privets and myrtles. I am glad to hear that some of them are still there. They were very beautiful.

When I was old enough I went to the village school, and at home played with my brother and two boys from the nearby cottage. We had wonderful games on Saturday afternoons in the goods shed which was closed then for traffic. There were plenty of things to play with: ropes, sack barrows and various tools which we made good use of, not forgetting to try anything edible found lying around, for instance locust beans, lovely dark brown sweet chews, and brown peas hard as iron. One of my favourite places of amusement was the signal box, high up and with windows all round from which one could view the surrounding countryside.

I could never pull the signals but was sometimes allowed to try a message on the telegraph machine. The booking office was a wonderful place where one could cadge gum, string and coloured leaflets advertising excursions to the seaside, and with the help of a few garden canes make a jolly good kite with a long tail of coloured papers. In those days of the Great Eastern Railway or later the London and North Eastern Railway, the trains were always regular and of course punctual to the minute.

Our day was governed by the times of the trains, one got up with the 7.30 am train, had breakfast with the 8 something coming in, my mother put on the potatoes when the 11.15 came down, and dinner was served after the 12.30 had gone up, and for me when small the 7.15 pm was my "bed train".

Lying in bed in a room facing the oncoming down trains, I could count the trucks on a goods train by the bumps over the level crossing, fifty usually. On foggy evenings there were different noises, fog signals going off, and weird sounds as engines slithered and spluttered on the frosty rails — "there's one stuck on the bank"! Sometimes there was a very special train, the royal train going down to Sandringham and then we would try and find a good spot, but not on the platform, from where we would try and get a glimpse of a royal passenger. We never did!

That reminds me that my father was also a railway child. He was to have been a carpenter but just as he was to be apprenticed, his father died. So instead he was sent to live with his guardian who was station master at Wolferton, the Royal Station for Sandringham. Here he lived for some time and had as a playmate none other than young Prince George (later George V) who loved the station works and the grease etc. It was my father's job to clean him up before he went home!!

Station masters and their families along the line were all friends, and so we would exchange visits and have parties. It was interesting to note that the station houses were usually built in the same style, so we almost always felt at home, though away. Going with my father and mother on trips to London or on holiday was always easy and comfortable fancying ourselves in a first-class carriage with foot warmers in winter as

Harry Butters, Elsenham Station Master centre with other railway staff and the crew of the last bus from Thaxted to Elsenham.

an added luxury. One thing however did worry me on those occasions was the fact that my father would get out of the train at various stations to have a handshake and a chat with the station master. I was always scared he would never get back into our carriage before the guard blew his whistle and we were off again!

When I was eleven they began to build the Light Railway to Thaxted and that was an interesting and exciting time. Every Sunday my brothers would get a trolley and we would go on the newly-laid rails as far as possible. Each week we advanced through Henham, then Sibleys and at last one day we got as far as Cutler's Green. That was the nearest I had so far got to Thaxted.

At last the railway was completed and officially opened with great celebrations, and when the train was running to and from Thaxted and Elsenham carrying passengers and goods then many changes were seen. The Rogers' horse-bus to Thaxted had made its last journey, and no longer was Sim Harvey, the usual driver, seen tying up his horse to our garden gate post. Now I often went to Thaxted on the train with my father when he went on business affairs with the shopkeepers and tradesmen there. Those visits were my first to this old town, and I was enchanted with the place. But I never thought I would one day be actually living there and joining in its life style, and teaching in the council school for nearly forty years.

Living at the Station House meant coming in contact with all kinds of people. Our house became a refuge for people perhaps waiting for a train to Thaxted, and my mother was always at hand with a cup of tea, or maybe first aid with Friars Balsam and a bandage for any of the men on the station. We often had relief clerks who came in for a "cuppa" and a chat, and my brothers who worked away as booking clerks would often bring home a friend for the weekend. It was rather like belonging to one big family, and I even became a shareholder of the L.N.E.R. by joining their Savings Bank. They gave jolly good compound interest and it was surprising how my savings grew from the sixpences put in during my childhood. When my father died in 1920 and my brothers gave up issuing travel tickets for the interest of growing tomatoes and chrysanthemums this money had to be withdrawn, and I ceased to be a Railway Child.

**Kate then added the following**

Since writing this, I have been reading some notes on the Butter's Family written by my sister, and am interested to find that my grandfather was really an experienced professional gardener. His brothers got bitten by the "Railway Bug" and became station masters and he gave up his profession and followed suit. Now comes the end of the cycle, for my brothers gave up their work on the railway, took up gardening and became nursery men growing tomatoes and flowers for market. The son of my youngest brother went to Writtle College, got his science degree and became interested in plant research.

So the great-grand son carried on where grandfather left off.

# ELSENHAM PAROCHIAL SCHOOL

## SOME OF THE THINGS THAT I REMEMBER ABOUT IT.

My name is Kate Butters and I lived at the Station House, Elsenham, where my father was the Station Master. I must have started school when I was four years old, and was taken there by my three brothers, often rather unwillingly I believe. For it was a good walk to the school, and the boys were always glad of a lift in any kind of horse and cart. But alas, I was scared of horses and would never ride behind one, even in a carriage belonging to Sir Walter Gilbey, the squire of Elsenham and a famous breeder of race horses.

I remember my first day at school, being made to climb the gallery steps in the Infants Room and sit right at the top, almost at the top of the world!! I soon learned to read and write and made steady progress from the "Babies" to "First Class" where I was given a picture book as a prize *"For intelligent answers in object lessons from Governess, Xmas 1905"*. I cannot now remember any of these objects, but I think these object lessons were a very important part of the curriculum, encouraging us to think and talk.

The Head of the school (Mr. R. Screen) was always called "Master", and his wife who taught the Infants with the aid of a pupil teacher was addressed as "Governess". She wore a spotless white shirt blouse with a stiff high collar, fastened by a gold safety pin, and always smelt cleanly of Lifebuoy Soap.

I preferred my mother's scent, which was Elsenham Lavender Water, made at Gilbey's Factory at Gaunts End. The lavender was grown there, gathered and processed by some of the villagers. It was beautiful and my Father always gave Mother a half-pint bottle for Xmas! Sorry about this digression, but it was worth remembering. I wonder how many people in Elsenham remember it.

The room was heated by an open coal fire, with an iron guard in front, on which we could hang our wet coats on rainy days. No mackintoshes for us or Wellington boots, but thick winter coats and strong boots, with perhaps buttoned cloth gaiters.

Playtime was spent in the small playground, in which was a lilac tree and a big laburnum which had a fascinating crotch where one could sit, and its old trunk was shiny with the polishing of young bottoms. There was also a very good three-sided shelter, with a dry floor and seats, all round and where we played singing games, the older girls teaching us younger ones. The favourites were "The Farmer's in his Den" "Bingo", "Poor Sally is a-weeping", "Roman & British Soldiers". One I have never seen in any book of games was "Draw a bucket of water, for a lady's daughter," etc. This was played by just four girls and began with a very dreary tune, but finished up with a very fast twisting round in a ring with arms linked round the waists.

After Standard One, I got promoted to Standard 2 in the "classroom" as it was always called, a room built on the back of the "Big Room" and with a teacher who came every day from

Bishops Stortford. She was always very smartly dressed and cared for her good clothes by putting away hat and coat (or cloak) in a big hat box on top of the cupboard. She would then protect her dress by putting on an immense white linen pinafore with flapping shoulder frills. However she managed to keep so clean and immaculate among a class of often grubby, smelly boys and girls I cannot imagine as I look back! She was a wonderful example of order and cleanliness to us, and later as a teacher myself, I tried to acquire the same pattern of order in my classroom.

Although the school was not a church school, we were often visited by the vicar and on special saints days we would all go up to the old Norman church on the hill for a service, with Master playing the organ for the hymns. Every morning for a short time, the whole school would learn and recite passages from the Bible. For example, "I am the Vine, ye are the branches", "I am the Good Shepherd", the story of the Nativity, etc., an excellent way of learning good English, and today I cannot bear to hear these extracts altered and spoilt in the new translations. How can they think they are improving the old language?

When the last day before the Christmas holidays came round, we were reminded to bring our "Nuts and oranges bag", for the squire's daughter, Mrs. Hine, would come and fill this calico bag with all kinds of beautiful nuts and two enormous oranges. Each child also was given a new, shiny silver three–penny piece and if you had been extra good or industrious you had TWO!!

From the "Classroom" and Miss Austin, I moved to the "Big Room" under the eagle eye of Master, moving up year by year until I reached Standard 4. It was then that Master suggested that I should sit for a scholarship to the new Herts and Essex High School for Girls in Bishops Stortford. My parents agreed and eventually I sat for the entrance exam, passed, and said "Goodbye" to the dear familiar village school in 1912. But even now, as a retired school teacher of eighty three, I still can look back with pleasure and gratitude at the many happy hours spent there. The small village school is a great thing in the life of any child and none should ever be closed.

Since writing this in 1983 I have remembered an interesting incident that must have happened in 1911 or 12 at that village school. One day, two strangers appeared in the playground and taught us the steps and sequences of the Morris dances called Bean-setting and Rigs of Marlow. This was the time of the great revival of Morris and country dancing in England by Mary Neal of the Esperance Club in London. Nearby in Thaxted, Mrs. Noel was being helped by Blanche Payling (of this club) to introduce the people of Thaxted to this dancing, the children were learning the old singing games, and she was using a book containing the tunes and instructions edited by Mary Neal. Many years later (say twenty odd years or so) I was playing these tunes and many others, for the Thaxted Morris Men, and had become the proud owner of that very same book, kindly given to me by Mrs. Noel. What strange coincidence! A link with Thaxted! I know now why those two tunes always seemed so familiar in an odd nostalgic way.

Sept 1989

# SWEETS AND TREATS.

I go to the sweet-shop now and have to give so many pence and even pounds for a few sweets, I look back to my childhood days before 1914. Then we could get four ounces of good boiled sweets for one penny. Of course they were not wrapped up in one or two layers of paper and fancy foil, but what matter? We usually had half that amount, all for a ha'penny, and they did not stay in our pockets long enough to get sticky. What marvellous things we got for our Saturday penny. There were twelve caramels or eight big round knobs of toffee called Tuffens or Treacle Dabs, and these were screwed in a square of paper twisted at the top, and were jolly good. On a hot day our choice was a Sherbet-sucker, a small bag of sherbet with a liquorice tube for sucking up the fizzy powder. The Winter Mixture included some warming ginger flavoured sweets, and Satin Cushions were delicately coloured sweets with fizzy centres. Black Jacks or Bulls-eyes were rather coarse black and white striped rounds and strongly flavoured with peppermint. I remember the flat shapes lemon-butters and the odd banana shapes of another kind of rum-flavoured boiled sweet. These toffees were not soft and chewy like those we buy today, but lasted quite a while and were good to crunch.

At the Fair we bought the brown striped treacly tasting rock. I don't think we ever spent our money on chocolate, that was too dear for us and did not last long enough anyway. I was once given some Edinburgh rock, and never forgot the wonderful texture taste and colour. Sometimes when my mother went shopping in Bishop's Stortford she would buy big thick sticks of liquorice from the chemists and cut off chunky pieces for us. Once I bought one or two big toffees each containing a tin lark's whistle which fascinated me until I drew in too sharper a breath and swallowed it. That meant being under strict, observation for some considerable time, but all was well, though no more bird-song for me. Lee's Soft Mixture was a lovely assortment of creams, fondants and marzipan in fascinating shapes and colours, not forgetting the beautiful strawberrys complete with green frill and stalk. If we went to our old Norman church on the hill for a little service on Holy Innocents Day, we were given a small bag of this dainty mixture. What a treat that was.

What about jelly-babies, and those flat sugar rounds with greetings and loving phrases on them, known as Cupid Whispers; and don't forget the dolly mixture, and the good old acid drop. We normally called these treats sweets, while to some children they were "suckers," and my cousins from the Fens always called them "dods." When I stayed with them in the holidays, we went "up town" on Saturday evening to buy our "dods" for Sunday. Sometimes we

*She was very fond of her family, and there was great excitement when Auntie Kate was to visit us.*

*She was a generous Aunt who took unusual presents, still greatly treasured, on her visits from Thaxted in addition, there were, of course, bags of sweets from Lee's Sweet factory. Later, girl friends were taken to be vetted.*

*My wife is pleased to say that she must have passed the test!*

*From Kate's nephew, Peter.*

made our own toffee, or brandy snaps. My sister would make "frumerty" of wheat and milk, or try to parch peas on the kitchen stove; and if they were not eatable at least they were amusing as they jumped about the room. As the winter drew near, the treats to look forward to were oranges, nuts of various kinds, of course chestnuts to roast by the fire, flat figs in their little wooden boxes and fat brown dates. All these came in time for Christmas, the greatest treat of all!

One really great treat during the year was of course the Sunday School treat in the summer when we were taken the two miles to Stansted Flower Show in farm waggons kindly lent with the horses and drivers by the farmers. We enjoyed the slow bumpy ride in the big creaky waggons drawn by huge cart horses decorated with shiny brasses and coloured braids knotted in their manes.

We wandered round the tents admiring the flowers and vegetables, and the mouth–watering cakes. Then we spent our money at the fair, on the swings or the roundabouts, or having a helpless go at the hoop-la, or a shy at the coconuts equally unrewarding. Then we gathered at a special tent where we enjoyed a lovely tea of sandwiches, slabs of cake and sugary buns, all washed down with mugs of milky tea. Later we made our way to the waiting waggons and were soon on the road home, tired, hot and grubby, but not too tired or weary to sing, and to say "Thank you" to those who had arranged the treat.

The winter treat was the Christmas party for the Sunday School children held in the Village Hall. It began with a lovely tea of good treats, and when all this was safely put away, then came games and a sing-song. We played "Nuts in May" and "Oranges and Lemons", and danced "Sir Roger de Coverly". At the end of the room was a tall Xmas tree, gaily decorated and laden with presents for everyone. When these were given out, we got into our warm coats and hats, and made our way home along the dark roads with the aid of our new electric pocket torches.

A very special treat at the village school at Elsenham was just before Xmas. We would be told to bring our bags for nuts and oranges on the last day of school. Every girl and boy had a calico bag made and kept during the year for this occasion. On this particular afternoon Mrs. Hine, daughter of Sir Walter Gilbey, of Elsenham Hall, and squire of the village, arrived with Xmas Fare. There were baskets of beautiful oranges, and nuts of all kinds. We held open our bags and soon they were filled with these huge oranges, brazils, almonds, chestnuts and cob nuts. But that was not all, for everyone of us had a bright shiny silver threepenny bit, and if you had been extra good or clever at your lessons, you had Two! What a lovely bag of goodies to take home for Xmas. The oranges were a real treat, for we only had them at this time of the year, and never so big as these, and the little silver coins were worth quite a bit in those days.

Another special treat was the Xmas Party at Elsenham Hall given by Sir Walter Gilbey. It was held in a room with the carpets rolled up and chairs placed round the room. At one end of the room was an enormous Xmas tree, beautifully decorated and laden with presents, complete with a dainty fairy doll right at the top.

26

One of the ladies of the family freed her fingers from her long white kid gloves and played the piano for us to dance "Sir Roger de Coverley", and we played the usual party games like "Hunt the Slipper", "Musical Chairs", and the old favourites of "Nuts in May" and "Oranges and Lemons". I remember the butler, wearing a big false nose, coming into the room carrying a large silver tray on which were raisins in flaming brandy, "Snapdragon", he called, and invited us to come and pull one out. I don't think I even dared try. Everyone was given a present from the Xmas tree, even the Mums and Dads, and finally there was a competition for a huge Xmas Stocking filled with toys or the fairy from the tree top. Imagine my surprise and delight when I won her. She was so beautiful, made of almost transparent wax, and I treasured her always, taking care not to sit with her too near the fire in case she melted away. To the children of today, these treats and sweets no doubt seem trivial and very inadequate, for they demand and often get so many and so much. But to us in those days they were the high-lights of the year, looked forward to so eagerly, enjoyed at the time and remembered afterwards with increased pleasure.

*When Kate was at the school during the war, and when there was an air raid, we was told to either run to the shelters or hide under the desks. So of course, we was really worried about Miss Butters. Now Teddy Foster, he said, "You don't want to worry, Miss Butters, 'cos if they drop the bombs and if it's got my name on it, you'll be the one to get it."*

*She said, "Well thank you very much for that!"*

# GAMES OF MY CHILDHOOD.

The seasons of the year follow each other in exact order, and so it seems do the seasons of games in a small child's life. Who decides when it is time to bring out that well-worn skipping rope which has been so carefully put away on a shelf in the wash house? Or is it time to hunt for your old solid red top keeping company with a precious piece of tile which you always used for a game of hopscotch. Of course it really was the weather that determined which game was to be played, for these were times in the early years of this century, when the roads and paths in the village were made up of gravel and broken

> *Kate actually remembered that the first car was a steam-driven motor car from Horham Hall.*

stones. So when it was wet weather there was MUD, and when the sun shone and dried up the mud, there was DUST. Yellow dust, and dust everywhere, on the grass verges, on the hedges, on your shoes, and clouds in the air when the occasional motor car came honking along at twenty miles an hour.

Hoops were for the cold frosty days, when the roads were hard and dry, and then the iron hoops of the boys made a pleasant noise as they trundled them by means of an iron slide. Some boys would put pig rings on their hoops and these added a jangling sound. The girls had to be content with wooden hoops of various sizes. Mine was a big one, and sometimes in my imagination it became a bicycle, which I longed to possess. I was to wait many years before I had a real one.

Skipping for the girls must have started when it was warmer weather, for having skipped your way to school on a good clean path, you could join a group of older girls with their long rope being turned by a girl at each end, and others standing by waiting their turn to run into the swirling rope. There were all kinds of singing rhymes to fit the different skipping sets, and one had to be quick to run in and out of the rope. The clever ones could skip in the double ropes which we called French skipping. And don't forget the "Salt, mustard, vinegar, pepper", in which the Pepper was skipped in double quick time.

Hopscotch was played on a plan of six squares drawn out on a level part of the playground, hopping and kicking the flat piece of tile from square to square in a sequence of movements till you kicked the tile out or on to a line, when you were out.

Quiet summer games were with marbles, when the boys played a game on the ground, with a small hollow near a wall, into which the marbles were rolled.

The girls used five green glass marbles taken from ginger beer bottles, to play

"Jinks". Some called them "five stones". The more chipped and rough the marbles were, all the better for the game, as they would not roll so much. This game could be played sitting on the ground, or on the hearthrug by the fire in the winter. This game had a very long sequence of things to do with your jinks, and hardly anyone could ever get to the end of it.

The whip-tops were of two kinds, the solid spinner and the smaller peg tops know as "fliers" as they could fly, and sometimes flew through a nearby window!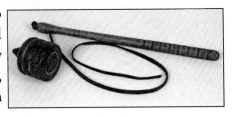

Indoors we had the lovely big humming tops started off by a length of string, or the pretty little wooden tops you could spin with a flick of the fingers.

I remember an interesting game the boys at the village school used to play in the winter. Just before twelve o'clock, one - the Fox - went out from class and disappeared. Later the rest of the boys - the Hounds - went off in search of the Fox. They must have run several miles for they didn't come back until we had been back in class after dinner. At last they returned, often muddy and breathless, but rosy-cheeked and bringing into the classroom lovely fresh air. They never got into trouble for being late for afternoon school, it was one of those things that just had to happen once or twice in the winter if the weather was suitable, and always on a Friday. "Master'" as we always called our headmaster, approved of this game, and allowed it to be played several times in the cold winter days. There were no organised games for boys or girls in those days and physical training was only just being introduced.

At home my brother and I had our games shared sometimes with two other boys. We were lucky to have a meadow in which our parents kept chickens, ducks, and pigs. The field had been used once by a man having greenhouses, so there were hills and hollow where he had dug out and changed the soil. In them we could make dugouts, or build houses or huts with wood from the hedges, thatching them with willow herb stalks which we cut from a nearby ditch. Once we made a lovely wigwam, but we wanted to have a fire in it, so unhappily it finished up as a great bonfire. My father built us a very good strong swing in the backyard, where we also had a "tee-ta-matorter." This is Suffolk dialect for a see-saw.

Indoors in the winter evenings, we amused ourselves with card games, Dominoes, Ludo, a ring board or a solitaire game. Do children play these today? Snap was a lovely noisy game which had to give place to a quieter "Drain the well dry". We had a set of Happy Families, not the Mr. Bone the butcher, but based on Alice in Wonderland, with the proper Tenniel drawings. Sometimes we made cut-out figures and jointed them with brass paper fasteners. You could make an acrobatic monkey in this way. Cat's cradles was another quiet game, until you came to the end when you sawed the string until it broke. My brother had two steam engines which were great fun, but the prize thing was the Magic Lantern. After a great deal of preparation, putting up the screen, getting the slides in order, and lowering the lights and so on, we invited Mother and Sister to come to the show. Usually just as they got settled, something went wrong and back to their needlework in the sitting room they would go. Getting everything ready took most of the time, and was perhaps the best part, for I'm afraid the performance seldom came up to scratch. At party times when we were a crowd, we played "Tip-it" with two teams; one with a coin to hide in one hand, and the others to call "Hands up" and try to find the coin. And of course no party was complete without Consequences. That always raised a laugh. Simple games, and no computers or electronics, but I guess they would not satisfy the child of today. What do you think?

---

*Kate said one day she could do with a hand in the garden, and anyway she was talking about someone to do this as a job. That day Melvyn was here and he offered to help. Now we were all talking about it and of course we were all very highly educated in those days. "In France they call them," says Kate, "I forget what they call them in France, what they call boys." Anyway, Kate gets the dictionary down and "Ah", she says, "It's called the 'garçon'!" So ever from then on Melvyn was known as the 'garçon'. Anyway, she said to me one day, "When 'garçon' comes ask him if he will just go round that garden and get those few weeds out." When Melvyn appears, she said, "Tell garçon we're ready to have the weeds out". She got him to go up there and under strict orders as to which he should pull out and which he should leave, which he really done, 'cause it really was not a good idea to cross Kate.*

*So the name 'garçon' remains.*

---

# SECONDARY EDUCATION.

Having won a scholarship from the village school, I went to the Herts and Essex High School at Bishop's Stortford in September, 1912, and with the aid of a bursary for the fifth year I stayed till July 1917.

I then went to Avery Hill Training College for two years.

> *Kate received several imposing volumes of poetry and literature as prizes for her work in English, French and Music.*

My mother had kept all my school reports; I am keeping the first and the last. Owing to World War One, the size of the report form had diminished. It also deprived me of two very fine volumes of poetry as form prizes; leaving me with a scrap of paper instead.

# WRITTEN FOR MAGAZINE TO CELEBRATE CENTENARY OF THAXTED SCHOOL 1880 - 1980

It was in the very hot dry summer of 1921 when I first came to teach in Thaxted Council School. I was given charge of Standards III and IV, who numbered around sixty boys and girls in one very large room. The desks were mostly of the old type, fixed tops and no backs and seating six children. There was nowhere to keep books etc, so these must be given out each morning and collected up again in the afternoon.

Just before I joined the staff, the school had been very sharply divided into Boys' Department and Girls' Department, but on the retirement of the Headmistress of the Girls' Department, Miss Archer who lived at Rose Cottage, the two were joined under the Headship of Mr. L. Bunting. This mixing of sexes was the cause of some amusing embarrassment at first, but soon settled itself. I was delighted with the atmosphere of the whole school; other members of the staff were friendly and helpful, and the real country children were a joy to be with. I was also a country child, spending my first school days in the small village school of Elsenham and spending many happy hours wandering in the fields and woods near my home. So we had common interests and I loved all the rare and

C Hannay and H Jeffrey

beautiful butterflies and wild flowers brought from West Wood, and not least the apples often scrumped from someone's orchard!

Among my first pupils were boys who are now grey-haired grand-fathers and retired senior citizens, but to me still the chubby rascal of nine or ten, vying with each other for the privilege of pushing my bike round to the back shed, for I was cycling in from Elsenham every day, and every day that year was a sunny day.

When winter came we heated the room with a great black tortoise stove which either got red hot and scorched the faces of those sitting within range; or if neglected as regard the stoking, would suddenly go dead on us. The playground was gravel except for a small asphalt path, so in wet weather my first job in the morning was to shovel up the mud from the floor. Some children walked long distances to school, from the Hydes, Cutlers Green and so on. No hot dinners for them, just some bread and cheese or a hot potato baked on the stove with water from the yard pump. When it grew dark on cold winter afternoons we had to light the oil lamps swinging above our heads. And for those who lived a long way out came the wonderful privilege of "going out early" to be home before dark.

Thaxted School Wall 1921

# THE DUNMOW FELLOWSHIP [FOUNDED 1921]

This was an idea to bring together teachers in the Dunmow area, to enjoy primarily, lectures from eminent men and women from the educational world; to talk over and compare their own experiences, successes and failures; and to enjoy socially, the companionship of old and young members of the teaching profession. Captain Cranmer Byng was, I believe, the real instigator of the idea. He felt that many teachers in the remote and rural districts found it a very lonely life; transport was difficult and one suffered from a sense of isolation. He stressed that not only should time be given to educational subjects, but there should be talks on art, music, drama etc.

The Countess of Warwick was interested in the scheme and offered the Barn Theatre at Easton Lodge for a lecture room for a week's summer school. She also opened her beautiful gardens and grounds for our recreation in the afternoons.

The Barn Theatre and the Countess of Warwick in the centre of the photo.

After morning lectures in the Barn, followed by a good lunch arranged under the expert eye of Mrs Cranmer Byng, we were free to socialise and enjoy these lovely gardens, walking around, sitting and chatting by the lake, or "just sitting."

If you should wander into the garden of H.G.Wells, who lived near, he would come out and shout, "who's for hockey?" and we would grab sticks and rush up and down his lawn hitting the ball if you got a chance, and getting redder and hotter every minute. It was summertime and mid-day!! I've had a grand strawberry tea one afternoon in his garden. I have never seen such an enormous bowl of strawberries!! I remember seeing there all the maps drawn by Horrabin for H.G. Wells' "Outline of English History".

During the week, for that was the length of the school, we had a special talk or lecture in the library of Easton Lodge, followed by a lovely tea in the marquee. It was a great chance to see and hear some of the most prominent people in the literary, art or political world. Another highlight of the week was an expedition to Stone Hall, a quaint stone lodge shut away in a grove of trees as a sanctuary for wild animals and birds. There was an interesting

**The Sundial of clipped box in Stone Hall, Easton Lodge**

sundial of clipped box, and the Countesses' Garden of Friendship. This was planted with flowers and shrubs given to her by her friends - all labelled and named (plant and giver) with pottery labels made by the Castle Hedingham potter.

Miss I.V. Cooper and K.B. In our "Cloche" Hats

One year we had Ben Greet Players giving plays from Shakespeare either in the Barn or in the gardens. These were very popular and were open to anyone in the district, as were the evening lectures. Some other names I remember were Granville Bantock and Rodney Bennet for music.

Transport was a difficulty, as very few teachers had a car in those days. So some of us cycled each day, others must hire a car. I forget what I had to pay for the course, but we felt it was a worthwhile effort and we enjoyed the week.

Later when the Barn was no longer available we used the Braintree Secondary School, but it was never the same.

# CHANGES AND HIGHLIGHTS IN THAXTED SCHOOL FROM 1925

In 1925 came a change of headmasters. Mr. Bunting retired and Mr. Jenner took over with a firm hand in more ways than one, and soon came many changes. He introduced gardening as an interest for the boys and soon we had flower beds and vegetable plots, a lovely lily pond and rockery and later even a greenhouse. With the girls I had a flower garden and an interesting herb garden designed in the shape of an Elizabethan Knot. From this they dried herbs for their cookery class at Dunmow and even crystallized the thick stalks of angelica.

We needed a piano and the Essex Education Committee said they would "give" us one, if we paid half the price. We had to have one at once and we were to earn money for our half by giving a school concert. So one arrived and after weeks of rehearsals, making of costumes and props etc., it really took place, well supported by parents and friends. These were always jolly occasions and if something or somebody went wrong it didn't matter one little bit! I remember choosing a boy with a wonderful crop of untidy curls and cheerful grubby face to play the part of an organ grinder, complete with a wonderful mechanical organ, kindly lent, and a monkey, just a stuffed one, only to come into the dressing room on the concert night to find him with a very close haircut and a clean face!! Where was my grubby organ grinder? There was also a great discussion and almost a free-fight between two small girls as to who went wrong in the Grand Chain. This so delighted Dr. Weller, Dr. Michael's father, that if we could ensure it happening on the second night he would have to come again!

Among the frequent visitors to the school was the Countess of Warwick, who came one day and gave a talk on "Kindness to Animals". At the end of the session she invited Mr Jenner to bring the senior children to have tea at Easton Lodge. This was arranged eventually a few days before the Easton Lodge Flower Show. So after a delightful tea of delicious sandwiches, strawberries and iced cakes in abundance, we were taken down through the park where Greenaway had his swings and roundabouts for the fair. The Countess shook the oily hand of Greenaway, hers in a white kid glove, and said, "Now Mr. Greenaway start up the engine and let the children have all the rides and swings they like". This after such a tea! Well, in spite of everything that would naturally happen in such circumstances, all had a wonderful time and lived to tell the tale.

Easton Lodge and Gardens

The next great change began at the end of July 1927 when remodelling of the whole school began. New floors were laid, lobbies enlarged and fitted with wash basins, new lavatories, windows added and the three separate departments merged into one. The big classrooms were divided by glass partitions, black-boarding put on the walls and shelves and cupboards

40

added etc. etc. We had two weeks extra holidays as work was not finished, but even when we did reassemble it was CHAOS. Central heating was still being inserted, so we tried to carry on work to the accompaniment of "clang, clang bang, rattle". Painters were still working inside so there was also the risk of someone falling over the ladders or landing in the paint pots. But at last all was finished and we all appreciated the great improvements.

In November of that year we did some tree planting in the playground. Each of the managers and the staff planted silver birch or prunus. The oldest girl and boy and the youngest child also planted their trees.

December 22nd saw the first issue of the school magazine, "Ours" with contributions from various classes and printed by senior boys. Has anyone got a copy hidden away?

Now we decided to have a good school badge. So we put the town's coat of arms, the crossed swords, fetterlock and the white rose of York on a red background, on a well shaped shield, and had them properly embroidered. The boys wore these on their own caps, and the girls had theirs on the front of sports tunics. These tunics were made by the girls in the needlework classes, black material with white braid trimmings and girdles. They looked very smart, and

were in preparation for the North Essex School Sports, which had their first meeting in June 1929 at Saffron Walden. This was attended by schools in the Walden area, and competition for shields and medals was great and very exciting. It was a wonderful day for the children and teachers, and well supported by parents and friends. We all yelled ourselves hoarse encouraging our boys and girls to do more than their best, and how proudly we arrived home with shields and medals. Considering that we had no good running tracks only the playground or a rough field, we put up a good show.

---

*Kate taught you when you were nine and ten. In her room was a pale wood piano which she played. She also played gramophone records. I remember once she was playing "Colonel Bogie", and even at eleven children knew bad words to it. Someone was singing loudly the rude words and she said, "What are you singing? He said, "Cabbages". So it went - "Cabbages da da da and the same to you!"*

*She read Tom Sawyer and Huckleberry Finn to us. I was amazed at the 1833 picture of Thaxted High Street, Town Street.*

*We made little wooden looms on which we wove ties. So we learned how to weave, we sang folk songs, all the folk songs, "Dashing away with a Smoothing iron", that sort of thing.*

*I don't think she was a severe teacher, but you get teachers who are naturally in control of the class.*

*A good teacher.*

# 1934 – MILK WAS ISSUED TO CHILDREN, $^1/_3$pt FOR $^1/_2$d

In May 1935 the school put on a pageant showing scenes of interest in Thaxted through the ages, beginning with the coming of the Saxon, Thane Wilaar, on a white pony lent for the occasion by kind parent. There were Saxon and Norman soldiers, a mediaeval fair under the Guildhall, a "hold-up" by the Thaxted Gang of Highwaymen, a dishonest baker dragged to the pillory for selling burnt bread, the visit of Queen Elizabeth to Horham Hall, the opening of the Light Railway, among the many interesting scenes. This meant a great deal of historical research for the script, and busy fingers with needles and cotton to make the costumes and jobs for the boys to make props. This was performed in Town Street, opposite and around the Guildhall in honour of the Silver Jubilee of King George V and Queen Mary.

The girls were now interested in spinning and weaving, making their own spindles of cotton reels and skewers, dyeing the spun wool with onion skins, privet berries and nettles etc. and weaving on simple homemade looms, scarves, belts and ties. Boys also wove their own ties.

July 1937. The senior children were taken to London where we visited the Tower of London and had a trip on the "Royal Daffodil" round the Port of London and saw the Docks etc.

October 1937. This was also a "highlight" for electricity was installed in school, so goodbye to those awful smelly swinging oil lamps, and welcome to our electric kettle for hot water for midday cocoa for children and tea for teachers, and an electric iron to use in the needlework classes.

**1938.** We became interested in glove puppetry and modelled the heads and dressed the puppets. Some wrote plays, the boys built a theatre and we all had a great deal of fun.

**1939.** Then of course came WAR and I have written elsewhere of some of my memories of those troubled years. I forgot to note that the Dinner Scheme began in December of that year, which of course was a boon to all. I cannot remember the price of a dinner, but the first cook had £1 per week.

**1946.** In May of this year children were brought in from the Lindsell and Broxted schools. One of the Broxted boys in my class of Standard V was Peter Smith who now comes to school talking of Road Safety.

**July 24.** This month saw FREE MILK and the last 1/2d was wrapped up and put in the school museum.

**1947** In this year my class was working on a scrap book of interesting things about the school and town to send to a small country school in South Dakota, U.S.A. where my second cousin was teaching. We had exchanged letters for some time, and some children had received lovely presents from the pupils there, who numbered less than ten altogether.
The school leaving age was now raised to 15 and we were waiting for an extra hut to be built to house these children.

Eventually it was finished and ready for use with beautiful science benches complete with bunsen burners but <u>no gas!</u> This was opened on April 21st by Mr. Primmer.

**1948 May 14th** Presentation to Miss Cooper on retiring after 50 yrs. of teaching.

**May 26th** Swimming instruction began at Saffron Walden baths.

**1949 July 21** Presentation of purse of money and autographs of subscribers to Mr. Jenner on his retirement as headmaster here for nearly twenty-four years.

**September 1949** We re-opened the school under Mr. Bennett as acting headmaster. In October I had to go to hospital for a major operation and did not resume duty until the following April when Mr. Westcott became our new headmaster.

Mr Jenner, centre, with A. Moore, B. Whyard and KB left

In September the Junior school was re-organized. Seniors waiting to go to Saffron Walden.

**December 15th** Party for Seniors to say goodbye to Thaxted and transfer to Saffron Walden Secondary School.

So ended the Autumn term 1950 and the last day of being an "all age" school. January 1951 saw the beginning of a Primary School.

> *She taught Nature Studies, taking us on nature walks in Walnut Tree Meadow where we explored the undergrowth and into the culvert.*

## WAR MEMORIES

In August 1939 I was enjoying a holiday by the sea, when I was suddenly recalled by Mr. Jenner, my headmaster and billeting officer for the town, to be at school to welcome and help in billeting evacuee children as war was threatened.

Two schools from London came complete with staff and shared buildings and of course books and apparatus with us. We used the Church Hall, Bolford Street Schoolroom, a room at the Rose and Crown, The Guildhall and rooms in the house next to the International Stores.

So began a hectic time, dividing up classes and moving from place to place, sometimes in school or in these rooms. Air raid shelters had been built in the yards but most were considered unsafe, so if the siren went it was "under the desks" for the children. "Get under the table, Miss Butters, get under the table," implored one of my boys, whether out of concern for my safety or for the fun of seeing me on his level I shall never know. But I remember the incident and when I meet him now in the street I wonder if he remembers it too. What extraordinary lessons we had in those days improvising and inventing all kinds of activities, teaching boys to sew on buttons and how to darn their socks, or patchwork for a class of girls I had in the Guildhall Council Chamber! One very cold winter's morning, when everywhere was covered with snow, this class was so cold that I borrowed a sledge and we had a lovely time across the Mill fields. That warmed us up and did us more good than long division!

These were hectic and disturbing days for us all, children and teachers. Great arguments and wrathful outbursts as pens and pencils disappeared and books were muddled up due to sharing desks and classrooms with the evacuees. Sometimes after an "all clear" it was our job to see some children safely home, only to find them following behind us on our way back "going shopping" they said! But fortunately we escaped bombing, apart from one or two scares and at last came peace. So eventually we were almost back to normal with our school to "we-selves" as we say in Essex.

**Having written this short piece, Kate must have decided to write more extensively. See the pieces that follow. Inevitably there is some repetition.**

*My husband was taught by Miss Butters. He told me she once rolled his shorts up and slapped him on the legs. "What did you do wrong?" I asked. "I don't know" he replied, "but I know I never did it again!"*

47

# MEMORIES OF A TEACHER IN THAXTED
## SCHOOL DURING WORLD WAR II.
### THE EVACUEES

It was August 1939, and I decided to have a seaside holiday in spite, or perhaps because, of rumours of war breaking out at any moment. But because my head-master, Mr. Jenner, was the billeting officer for Thaxted and all the Staff were to be in readiness to help in case of trouble, I had to give him my seaside address and be prepared to set off for home if I received a telegram from him. I enjoyed a few days with my relations and friends, and then one day as I was relaxing in a lovely hole in the sandy beach, that telegram arrived!

So I packed my bags and returned home, and at once made my way up to the school. Here preparations were being made

to receive evacuated children from London. There were official cards on which to register each child, and more important of all lists of kind people willing to take on one, two, or more children and give them a home and there were cases and cases of emergency rations for the children to take to their foster homes.

The day when the first coach load of children arrived was a

beautiful summer's day, but very hot for these children bundled up in many clothes, and carrying various packages and of course the gas mask box. They were hot, thirsty, grubby and bewildered and I shall always remember one small child of five probably, sitting on the floor of my classroom, her sad little face with tears trickling through grime and chocolate smears. **(This was Shirley Archer only 3yrs old then, but whom Kate met again in Church one Sunday in July 1983.)**

We had to fill in these official cards with their names, ages, etc., and the schools and district from which they came. They were then given rations of corned beef, dried milk, and Bourbon biscuits among other things. I remember the biscuits for it was ages after the war was over, before I could face them again! The children were then given over to those kind people who had offered to take them in, and we hoped they would settle down and be happy in their new homes, while we prepared ourselves to welcome another contingent the following day

The next day we waited for another coach load of children, but to our consternation we were faced with a party of "pink labels", pregnant ladies, instead of children. That caused some difficulties as they were not so welcome as children. But as far as I can remember they were all found homes. That reminds me of one incident that was to be stamped on my mind for a long time. One mother, with a very young baby, could not be placed anywhere; so she was made comfortable with blankets and pillows in one corner of a classroom, and there must have been hay and straw as well for it was just another "Nativity -

No room in the inn." Mr. Hannay, the school caretaker, kept a copper of water boiling away in the school yard, for washing the nappies, and we kept her going with milk for the baby and food for herself, until we could find her a home.

In July 1939 most small cottages in Newbiggen Street chiefly and elsewhere in the town had been

condemned, and the occupants moved into new Council Houses at Magdalen Green. These empty cottages were now used to billet evacuated mothers and their children. Thaxted people gave or lent tables, chairs, beds, pots and pans, etc., and tried to make these cottages comfortable for the strangers. But they had no light except candles and oil lamps, open range cooking stoves and of course the "loo" at the bottom of the garden! So they found it difficult to adapt themselves to their new surroundings and often came up to the School with their complaints to Mr. Jenner, the Billeting Officer. He did his

50

best to try and smooth out their difficulties, but sometimes his patience would be severely tried, in particular by one Irish woman who turned up regularly every morning. In the end the only reply could be, "Well, if you're not happy Mrs. So and So you will have to go back to London, I've done my best to help you". Then she would relent and smother him with gratitude, and almost kisses, for all he had done. There were also, of course, complaints from some foster parents, where the children were upset, frightened and homesick. But gradually everyone settled down to the new mode of life, and most children enjoyed their new home the country. Some families even settled down for good and are still here.

Years afterwards I have been visited by many of these children, now grown up of course, who always greet me with: - "Don't you remember me? I used to be in your class". Three sisters came last year and one thanked me for teaching her to sew and said, "I've been sewing and making things ever since". I also met the brother of the sad little girl and when he told me his name I remembered her and told him how she had looked, he laughed and said, "I must tell old Shirley, she'll love that".

They all loved Thaxted and said that spite o' it being war those years spent here were the happiest of their lives.

> *Kate Butters had this wonderful sense of observation and a wonderful memory. She wrote as she spoke, in a strong Essex accent. So you can almost hear her speaking as you read her words.*

# SCHOOL DAYS DURING WORLD WAR II

Having settled the children and mothers into their foster homes, we now had to think about accommodation for the children for their school days. We had requisitioned several buildings for this use, the Church Hall, Bolford Street School room, the Council Chamber in the Guild Hall, an upper room in the Rose and Crown and a room in the house next door to the International Stores now owned by Mrs. Pearson. The teachers from the London Schools had arrived and time tables were drawn up sharing these buildings and the school premises between the locals and the evacuees, mornings in odd buildings school in afternoons and reversing.

There were often great difficulties and commotion over sharing books and apparatus, etc., but we had to overcome or ignore all this, and work for the best. Lessons were often very different and unorthodox. I had a class of senior girls in the old Guild Hall Council Chamber, crowded round one table with little room to write. So we made up various mental games, read lots of books and stories, did some patchwork pieces for a bedspread and talked a lot!

One morning in the very cold snowy winter of 1940 (?) I arrived in this old draughty room to find some girls in tears – they were so cold and miserable. So we got a sledge of mine and spent most of the morning sledging down the Mill Meadows, and at least we were warm and happy! It was often very difficult to know how to keep children interested when in odd places.

One day in Bolford Street School room I taught, or tried, a class of boys how to sew on buttons and how to darn their socks. I thought they might find it useful when they got into the army. Perhaps they did, but I shall never know.

When the siren went for alerts, it was "Get under the desks" if we were in school. "Get under the table, Miss Butters, get under the table," implored one of my boys, whether out of concern for my safety or for the fun of seeing me on his level I shall never know. But I remember the incident and when I meet him now in the street I wonder if he remembers it too. We had no shelters that were bomb-proof, they even let in the rain! With my class in the Guildhall we had to go down stairs, cross the street and stand or crouch on a ladder in the passage of the same house where the infants had a room with Miss Cooper.

Soldiers were stationed in the town at this time and used a room in the Guild Hall next to mine for their leisure time. When we had our door open in the summer time because it was too hot and stuffy, you can guess I had plenty of advice and offers of help from them. It all helped to make life a little amusing in those dreary war days.

When it was the local children's turn to use their school, then there were shouts of indignation and dismay as books, pencils, etc., were missing from their desks. The classrooms often overcrowded and it was not easy to keep account of who should be there. We had girls from Dr. Barnados Home evacuated to Horham Hall, and several times two or three of them went missing, and once they managed to get away almost to Ford End before being rescued and brought back!

There were also some very small boys from there, who had to be herded together in the afternoon, and delivered to Mr. Barrett's taxi. We should have had a sheep dog on watch, for though we kept an eagle eye on them, one would disappear and be on his way to London, via the Walnut Tree Meadow, with a penny in his pocket! They were past masters at disappearing acts!

It certainly was an experience to be a teacher in those times, for there were many different jobs for us and all kinds of tedious regulations about seeing children to their homes after school. I remember taking some up the Bardfield Road, delivered them safely, and turned round to get myself home when I was overtaken by some of the same children "Going shopping down the town"! they said gaily in answer to my query.

In spite of many arguments and complaints on both sides we made friends with the evacuated teachers, and found them ready and willing to co-operate. Some even joined us in fire-watching in the John Ball Chapel over the North Porch of the church and we spent many eerie nights there with the bats flying around us.

One teacher coming to join us from her billet in Newbiggen Street wrapped in her eiderdown and various blankets was challenged by the soldiers as she took the short cut through the Swan Yard, where they had their headquarters. But they let her pass though she looked like a cross between an Eskimo and a Russian; and also had a weird Welsh accent and an equally odd Welsh name!

Later on, when many children were taken back to London by their parents, most of the teachers went with them, and the rest of the children were put in classes with our own. One teacher, Miss Powers, did stay for good and became a permanent member of our staff until her retirement.

## A TRIBUTE BY BRUCE MUNRO

*Kate has been a part of Thaxted for so long, 81 years, no less, arriving here at the age of 22. The town is diminished by her death. Her arrival here as a teacher in 1921 was certainly Thaxted's gain, since her contribution to the life of this town was to extend far beyond the school, and influence both young and old in many ways.*

*To put her time scale here into perspective, she was appointed by Mr. Bunting, who was headmaster from 1895 to 1925. When he was appointed, the school now nearly 125 years old, was only fifteen years old, nearly new, and so her contemporaries reach back to teaching in the time of Queen Victoria.*

*Kate rode to school on a Raleigh bicycle and was always dressed in country tweeds and flat heeled shoes. She was by common consent an exemplary teacher, one whose authority was not questioned.*

*I believe she taught me in the 9-10 year, or it may have been the next year. The equipment in her room included a lightwood cased*

55

piano which she played beautifully and to which we sang and learned the lovely English songs and folk songs, things like "My bonny lies over the ocean", "Bobby Shafto" and many more - so we have to thank her for knowing all the good songs.

In what might have been an extra-curricular activity, we learned to weave. We had simple, small, looms, with no moving parts, on which we wove ties - which we then wore. Kate also showed us how sheep's wool was spun.

As well, she played gramophone records - 78's which were then the latest. I remember her enquiry of a pupil the words we were singling to Colonel Bogey. One particular word, soldier's language, was I suppose, offensive. He answered "cabbages", which seemed to satisfy her although I'm sure she knew the truth! On this same gramophone we learned the country dances. She also introduced us to the loveable scarecrow Worzel Gummidge amongst, I imagine, other perhaps more important works.

Kate taught Nature Study and we sometimes walked in Walnut Tree Meadow to study flora and fauna in the great hedge and the stream which it concealed, and she knew all the plant names and much more.

In the War, when the school had to accommodate evacuees, we were taught in venues outside the school, including the Guildhall, Bolford Street Schoolroom, the Church Hall, the first floor of the Rose and Crown, and what is now Crossways Tea Rooms* - all of which involved Kate. And she had taught in all those places. (*no longer a teashop, but a private residence.)

Outside school, I think even when quite young we were welcomed into the shop at Church House to chat to both Kate and Arthur, who might be at his great loom weaving lengths of beautiful material. And I know her style and flair, and taste, which made Church House such a place of character, influenced us all.

And then, of course, she was the official accompaniment for the Morris, and on Bank Holiday Mondays the dancers emerged from Church House led by Kate playing superbly on her accordion the Morris tunes which were so familiar to the people of Thaxted.

She remained active in retirement, still playing for the Morris and country dancers, gardening, needlework and much more, and through all the years she warmly welcomed those of her pupils who called to see her, both locals and certainly the former evacuees who sometimes called.

I wouldn't say she was sentimental, she called a spade, a spade, but she certainly enjoyed reminiscing.

Kate had a long and fulfilled life and there are many of us who enjoyed a Thaxted childhood, have much for which to thank her.

Kate: Teacher, Musician, Artist. She will be missed, and certainly remembered.

The Boys from Thaxted School - date unknown

# THAXTED DISCOVERS AMERICA. 1943

*"Thaxted, a little mercate towne seated very pleasantly upon an high rising hill."*
So wrote William Camden in 1610 of one of the quaintest and loveliest little market towns of England. And in 1941 it is still a beauty spot very little spoiled by the race of time and industry, and still having a mediaeval charm, due largely to its beautiful church high on the hill, smiling benignly down on the timbered and thatched houses clustered around it, like children clinging to their mother's skirts; and to the Guild Hall, looking as though it had stepped straight from a picture in a fairy tale book. This hall was built in 1485, just before Columbus discovered America, and nearly five hundred years were to pass over its gabled roofs, five hundred suns had to warm its timbered and plastered face, and many generations of children were to play on the flagstone forecourt under its old council chamber, before Thaxted was to discover America, or more truthfully, the Americans.

One sunny day in 1942 another group of children were playing in that same forecourt, skipping and singing to their steps: ‑

*A house to let, no rent to pay,*
*Knock at the door, and runaway"*

War clouds over‑shadowed their games, for they were snatching a brief break from lessons given, not in their schoolroom, but in that same old council chamber where years before, cutlers had held their guild meetings and the Mayor of Thaxted had tried his prisoners and condemned them to the little cell underneath the building.

Evacuated children from London were sharing their own country school, so half the day was spent by some of them in this quaint old building with its crazy stairs, sloping floors and tiny leaded windows. On this day, the skipping and the singing suddenly stopped, and eager girlish faces peered round the great oak pillars which supported the first storey, at a queer little motor car coming down the hill by the church, driven by a man in a khaki uniform of an unfamiliar pattern, with a still queerer cap upon his head.

It was the first Jeep Thaxted was to see, and the old town settled back under the shadows of her beautiful trees to watch the newcomers invade the place, race up and down the streets in these snorting little chariots, roar overhead with their bombers, take possession of her pubs, and captivate the hearts of the children with their gifts of chewing gum. Oh! marvellous plenty in a land starved of sweets! "Got'ny gum chum?" was the slogan of the day, and many an unsuspecting G.I. was held to ransom by daring urchins for one piece of spearmint.

Three miles away at Debden, the aerodrome was taken over by the 8th. Air Force, and joy was great in Thaxted when a

Christmas Party was announced and all Thaxted children were invited. A ride in an army truck, more gum on the way from the driver, films at the cinema, sweets, presents, and ice cream. I remember vividly, one youngster who stripped off his jacket, rolled up his sleeves and got ready to attack anything in the eating line! And oh! boy those iced cakes!! We grown-ups, who were fortunate enough to be there, had nearly forgotten such delicious cakes ever existed, and these youngsters had never known of their existence!

So gradually Thaxted got to know her American boy-friend, learned to say "O.K.", to chew gum, and to jump out of the way when jeeps came tearing around the corner of the street by the church wall. This was the "target for to-night," and in the local "News and Views", a monthly bulletin was issued, describing the "War of the Wall", and the latest developments in the breaking down of that same wall by the Jeeps and trucks, and the building up again by the church clerk, who is a bricklayer by trade.

Some sunny days, the Yanks, as we indiscriminately called them, made a more peaceful use of it, sitting along it to rest in the course of a route march, drab line of khaki figures with unfamiliar steel helmets decorated with flaming red poppies picked from the wayside banks.

Then one day, to an old 15th. century house, opposite the church, came a letter bearing strange writing and gay foreign stamps. A letter from America, fore-runner of many more to come, letters from children in a small rural school in South

Dakota, inviting the children of Thaxted County School to become their pen pals, and to write of their homes, games, hobbies and so on. So several very stilted and stereotyped letters were written to strange children with stranger names, packed in one bulky envelope and sent off with great excitement. Then days and days of waiting, until back came the first answers, and soon the ball was well rolling. Photographs were exchanged, and odd coins and small presents sent backwards and forwards as souvenirs. Later came magazines from the U.S.A. making our mouths water with their marvellous pictures of delicious foods, and giving us an insight into their mode of life, their clothes, houses, games etc.

This interchange has been going on for some time now, and this year a fresh batch of letters arrived from another small country school in South Dakota. A new set of children have answered these and so more chains of friendships have been forged between the children of the two countries.

Our children were interested in the differences of speech, names, crops grown on the farms, foods and commodities. So we thought it a good idea to compile a Scrap Book of various interesting things in our English every-day lives; articles about our currency and the prices of things, common birds and flowers, our own historical surroundings, notes on our school, our canteen, our industries and amusements which were rather unique, and include sweet-making, costumes and properties for the theatre, hand-loom weaving, colour photography of models for illustrations for books and Morris and country dancing, which forms a popular holiday feature of this old town. The children wrote their articles, drew and painted their pictures, collected their stamps, sweet and cigarette wrappers, made up the scrap book and bound it with covers decorated with the coat of arms of Thaxted.

This was a project for the term, and when finished was packed up with a small hand-woven scarf for the youngest pen-pal of six years, and a hand-made tie for the only other boy brave enough to write. We hope of course that the school in South Dakota will enjoy our effort, and send us a similar book in return. There is so much that could be done to increase the friendship between the two countries.

Many mornings, when school assembles, you can see boys and girls proudly clutching letters from America, showing off birthday cards or valentines sent by their friends, and giving away much-coveted stamps for collections. Some girls sport American hair-bows and clips, and one wears a beautiful woolly sweater knitted for her by her pen-pal. This girl is also the envy of her class for she is making a charming summer frock from two chick-feed bags, sent from a farm in South Dakota. In this instance too, the mothers have written to each other, a truly grand idea.

And so in these varied and devious ways has the sleepy little old town of Thaxted discovered America and her people.

———————————

**A copy of this little story was sent to U.S.A. for publication in one of their magazines.**

*5/13/71*
*Dear Miss Butters,*

*I return this essay reluctantly as you suggested, without being able to tell you personally that my husband and I enjoyed reading it. Thank you for sharing it with us. You shared it with us. I would like to share it with some others in my small city: possibly with some of the students in one of the schools.*

*Certainly with a friend or two for whom it might mean something as it did for us.*

*I wish I knew how to have it published in some way, but this is not my area, or am I acquainted with THE PRESS people. If you can have a copy made in your library, or somewhere, maybe you would mail it to us so we can share it.*

*Thank you for pleasant conversation - you and your partner.*

*Best of luck to you both,*
*Sincerely,*
*(Mrs) Betty Menaken*

# ESSEX EDUCATION COMMITTEE.

*Your Ref.*

_____

.

## MID-ESSEX DIVISION.

_____

*My Ref.* R/C

W. C. PRIMMER, M.A., M.Ed.,
Divisional Education Officer.

------------------------

Telephone: Chelmsford 4421

DIVISIONAL EDUCATION
OFFICE. SPRINGFIELD DUKES,
SPRINGFIELD GREEN,
CHELMSFORD.

21st September, 1959

Dear Madam,
Thank you for your letter of the 15th of
September, from which I am sorry to learn that
you wish to resign your appointment on the staff
of Thaxted County Primary School as from the
31st of December 1959.

I should like to take this opportunity of
thanking you on behalf of the Managers and the
committee for the service you have rendered
since you were first appointed to the school in
1921.

Yours truly,

*W. C. Primmer*

Divisional Education Officer,
Mid—Essex Division.

Miss K. Butters,
Thaxted County Primary School,
Near Dunmow
Essex.

# ESSEX EDUCATION COMMITTEE.

_____

*Your Ref.*

## MID-ESSEX DIVISION.

_____

*My Ref.* R/SC

W. C. PRIMMER, M.A., M.Ed.,
Divisional Education Officer.
------------------------
Telephone: Chelmsford 4421

DIVISIONAL EDUCATION
OFFICE. SPRINGFIELD DUKES,
SPRINGFIELD GREEN,
CHELMSFORD.

7th January, 1960

Dear Miss Butters,
        Thaxted County Primary School

At a meeting of the Managers of Thaxted County
Primary School held on 27th November, 1959, the
Head-master reported your resignation from the
staff of the school.

The managers placed on record their appreciation
of the services that you have rendered to the
school and have asked me to write to you on their
behalf thanking you for all the work you have
done for the school and the children in it, since
you were first appointed to the staff of the
school in 1921

I should like personally to join with the
Managers in wishing you a very long and happy
retirement.

                Yours sincerely,
                *W. C. Primmer*
        Divisional Education Officer,
            Mid—Essex Division.
Miss K. Butters,
Church House, Thaxted.

Kate was presented with a small notebook when she retired from Thaxted School in which staff and pupils had written these words.

# A COLLECTION OF KIND WORDS

*With fond memories and sincere wishes for a long and happy rest.*

*"Cor it makes ya sweat don't it?"* **(See anecdote on the next page)**

*Hoping to see you at the sea-side sometimes - Bett & Reg Wescott*

*Now for the Joy of Craftsmanship and many happy years – Jack Putterill*

*May you now conquer all the new fields that will open to you. Best wishes – Margaret Hunter*

*May you enjoy many sunny hours on the "seat at the end of the garden." Peter and Donald join me in wishing you years of peace and contentment. – N.J. Bone.*

*With all good wishes for a long and happy retirement and with happy remembrances of our work together from 1925 – 1949. E L Jenner - Head*

*Thanks for the memories – especially of the laughs!*

*"Little bit o' truck in me oiye" "We're widders we are"*

*"One of the REAL Noopshies" "'cept me feet do goo so 'oigh."*

*"Loiza's gorn wrong miss." "..... and we've only got eight saucers."*

*"Wot! No more sputters, Behind the shutters? Adieu, Miss Butters!"*

*Many thanks for all your good influences in the school – especially that of good taste.*

# FROM A TRIBUTE GIVEN BY SYBIL COLLINGS - 17TH MARCH 2003

*When Kate retired from Thaxted School she was delighted to be able to devote herself to her many other interests. With her good friend Margaret Hunter, she set off to Pottery classes at the Chelmsford Technical College, being taught by the eminent potter Jo Constantinedes. Enduring symbols of Kate's determination and dedication to the task in hand, abound in the house. Cups, bowls and plates have been in constant use for forty years to my knowledge! Pictures crafted by Kate and rugs and fabrics woven by them both adorn the house, and in odd corners clay faces gaze out at you - all examples of Kate's determination to master a craft and produce really useful and often, beautiful objects to use.*

*I have had many opportunities in the last few years to understand her great and deep knowledge and love of literature. Appropriate quotations popped out for most occasions. Her mind was always intellectually sharp - she was ever curious to learn about new things and kept up with current affairs by listening to the Five o'clock programme every day.*

---

*Kate cared about the progress of all her pupils. When Teddy Foster fell behind with his grasp of maths, or more accurately arithmetic, Kate suggested he stay behind after school for half an hours' extra tuition.*

*After some days of this, as the time was about up, Kate asked Teddy how he was getting on.*

*"Not too badly, miss, but Cor it makes ya sweat don't it!"*

# SOME MEMORIES OF BEING MUSICIAN (IN CHIEF) TO THE THAXTED MORRIS MEN.

For many years I had been interested in the Thaxted Morris Men - helping Mrs. Margaret Hunter, the Squire's wife, to make their waistcoats, in place of baldricks, of glazed floral chintz trimmed with red woollen braid and fastened with toggles. Also making baldricks and bells for a team of boys. But I never dreamed I would have the difficult task to play for their dancing. Father Jack Putterill was musician at this time using chiefly a "squeeze box" which was rather frowned upon by the powers that be. But to play the whistle out of doors against a noisy crowd require great breath and the accordion was so much easier. However, in 1938 Father Jack was appointed to a living in Plaistow, and so what about the music for the team? One member of the team, no names, said to me, "You must do it. Get a squeeze box and get cracking!" "I can't do that", says I, but I had to go and buy a small Hohner accordion and try my luck. The keyboard was no trouble, but the wind and the bass keys were new to me. Then, as there were only eight bass keys for chords, which meant only three keys in which to play, I had the job of transposing all the tunes wanted by the team into one or other of these keys G, F and C (key G became the favourite and I think the easiest to fit the chords to). I then had to learn the tunes and fit the bass chords, all out of my head. Now I had to spend a great deal of time not only practising the tunes but learning how many A's, B's and capers, etc., not forgetting the "once to yourself" as I sometimes did! And how to play to their dancing which was most important! This meant going to their practices in the Church Hall mostly on Sunday afternoons or Monday evenings, no matter what kind of weather. In the winter - jolly cold for the fingers.

At first, when playing for them out of doors at fetes, etc., or in the streets here, I had to rely on my music copy, and I would get someone to act as music stand. But that was not always very helpful as they tended to forget their purpose in life at the moment, and turn round to look at the dancers or talk to friends. So though I found it difficult at first, I made up my mind to learn all the tunes off by heart. What a task! But I was in the job long enough to do this more or less. It meant I could watch the dancers and make a much better job of playing. It was old William Kimber, dancer and musician from the Cotswolds, who said, "You must play for the dancers not the audience".

I enjoyed playing for the team most of the time, tho, I suffered from nerves as the Squire, Alec Hunter would sometimes put on a new dance, whose tune I was not completely sure of, and also at a most important event.

My most terrifying experience was in Coronation Year, where they were dancing at the Mecca - an enormous ballroom, the team coming out from one corner and little me creeping out from another, hoping and trusting we should meet in the right place, and with the music, a newish tune and dance of course, just right for the team. I was always glad when Clifford the Fool was dancing around the team, for if I forgot the tune or played the wrong A or B he would sing it out and I could pick it up again. It can be quite a terrifying feeling, knowing you are the only source of music. You must not put a note too much or leave one out, or you will destroy the rhythm of the dance. I must say the team were always very long suffering and never bullied me. Perhaps they didn't dare!

Maurice Heard and John Munro, aged 9yrs, dancing Shepherd's Hey. Arthur Caton's first pupils

We went dancing at all kinds of events, large and small, very public or quite intimate. Regarding this last, we were putting on a small display, for a local party of W.I. members in a very pleasant garden. Soon someone said "Now let's do a stick dance" but no one had remembered to bring the bag of sticks! However, in the garden was a derelict row of runner beans with sticks - so - they were pulled up and the dance went on.

During the war we still danced in the Bull Ring on Bank Holidays, for people said, "Do dance and cheer us up." So we did, and sent our collections to the King George's Fund for Sailors.

After the war we got going again and tho' we had lost several members of the team we gained some new young ones. Later Father Jack was back in Thaxted as its Vicar, so we played together for the country dancing and Russell Caton later joined us with his fiddle. But I still played alone for the Morris.

One highlight was the Festival of 1952 when we had a grand procession of dancers from Rails Yard down the town, led by the King and Queen on horseback, and the streets swept clean before them by the "Sweeping Boys"; I forget their proper name. The musicians led by William Ganniford from Cecil Sharp House and others, had a high place in a lovely old farm waggon in the Market Place. It was a great event, and I enjoyed playing with those professionals. I continued playing for the Morris until I had a major operation, and afterwards did not feel up to the mark, even a small instrument is quite heavy to hold, and as we now had fiddlers and sometimes another accordion, I decided to retire gracefully and hang up my musician's jacket in the lumber room. I still have my accordion, but having broken my left wrist two years ago, cannot now hold the instrument and work the bellows and the bass keys, and get any rhythm in my playing as I used to. However, the world now seems full of accordions and musicians, so why bother?

I did my bit in those early days and kept the Thaxted Morris Men dancing, when they might have given up for want of a musician.

> *There was one Sunday afternoon, Arthur, Kate and myself (PK) sat in the front room, having a cup of tea and these two people came out of the church. They looked a bit 'arty crafty' sort of people and they looked across the road and saw that Arthur's window had a bit of crafts in it. This woman come up and tapped on the glass. She kept tapping Kate mouthed to her, "We're CLOSED!" So, this woman still waves and kept on her gestures and all that. So, Kate again said "WE ARE CLOSED". Arthur and me, we thought she's going to keep on. So, she did, she kept tapping on the glass bold as anything. So me and Arthur, feeling very brave 'cause we were brave young men anyway, got up and went and stood in the passageway. This left Kate to the ordeal. At which Kate goes to the door. She said "Yes?". This American said "Hi, we're Americans, from America," she said "We're 'arty crafty' people." "Yes", Kate said, "I suppose you're 'Arty' and you're 'Crafty', and WE ARE CLOSED!" Me and Arthur clutched ourselves together and thought how brave we were to run away!*

72

# MUSIC IN MY LIFE

I have vague recollections as a podgy toddler of three sitting on my sister's lap as she sat playing at the piano, and having my fat fingers pressed on the white notes to play "Three Blind Mice". Later of course she gave me lessons, and though I was very lax at really practising, I did manage to play simple pieces. When my sister had singing lessons I had to play her accompaniments and that encouraged me to work harder and improve my playing. We both used to play for the dances in our local village hall, and I had great fun playing vamping chords to the music of a concertina so well played by the man who looked after the birds in the aviary of Sir Walter Gilbey who lived at Elsenham Hall.

Our Sunday evenings at home were sometimes given over to music; a sing-song with friends from the village joining us; a solo perhaps by one brother or my sister, and even one by my father, and of course part-songs by all. It was all very low-brow but all the same most enjoyable. My mother used to play hymns to us on Sunday mornings if we were not going to church, and these would be out of the Sankey Moody book with the jolly tunes that we loved. She knew one by heart and we would sometimes hear this as she went near the piano, "Work for the night is coming"!! At the village school we were taught the old songs, like "Hearts of Oak", "The Minstrel Boy", and "The British Grenadiers" and so on, while in the playground we sang and played our favourite singing games, "The farmer's in his den", "Bingo", and "Poor Mary is a-weeping". Sometimes we went to a concert in the village or took part in it, but that I'm afraid was rather low-brow. These were the days before radio or even the gramophone, but I do remember being very excited at hearing a phonograph which played "The Departure of the Troopship" with great gusto.

At the high school I learned more of the theory of music, and the music teacher would play to us and explain the fugue for example, and tell us about the orchestra and all its instruments. The first musical instrument I bought was a mandolin, a lovely thing but I could do little with it. I then tried a small ukulele and later a banjolele. (A cross between a Banjo and a ukulele) Then I got interested in folk dancing and played the lovely dance tunes on the piano and trying then on a whistle or recorder. Now I took up the viola to join in the church orchestra, but later changed to the cello which I had always been secretly interested in but never thought I would ever own one, much less ever play one. With the help of Father Jack I did struggle with it and enjoyed playing though not at all well perhaps. It was great fun playing together, for we were all beginners and sometimes one member would be wading through a different piece of music. In this way we got an

*And as a particular tribute to Kate, Bobbie Ritchie played Kate's accordion (or her "Squiffer" as Kate referred to it) during the Morris tribute, in the Churchyard, to the Morris Men's farewell dance - Bonnie Green Garters. Her love of music never left her and those of us who were privileged to celebrate her 100th Birthday, will remember her entertaining us by playing Courante by Handel on her beloved piano.*

introduction to the music of Purcell, Handel, Byrd and others of that time. I always enjoyed hearing the choir sing madrigals, and the Bach chorales in church were a great joy to me. While in the choir and orchestra we performed "Dido and Aeneas" and even had a "crack" at parts of "L'Allegro" and "Il Penseroso" which were much more difficult and needed more practice than we had time to it. We even played in Great Bardfield Town Hall.

When Father Jack left us for Plaistow I took on the job of playing for our Thaxted Morris Team using a small piano accordion. This meant a great deal of hard work transposing tunes, learning to fit the bass chords, controlling the wind and also remembering the sequence of the dance. But I really enjoyed it when I could memorise the tunes and watch the dancers and become one with the team. I also played for country dancing, though sadly it meant that I had to give up dancing myself. I think I enjoyed this playing more than the cello, as I never seemed to have neither the time nor the inclination to practice and the resulting noise rather put me off! Now I have my piano and plenty of time to play it, and to discover all sorts of jolly "Courantes" of Handel that I had never attempted before. Sometimes I get out my accordion and play some of the beautiful Morris tunes.

*Kate's early days in Thaxted were greatly influenced, as were many others, by Conrad and Miriam Noel. She went to church and helped Miriam to do the flowers in a style which was as near as possible to their natural growth.*

# "DOING THE FLOWERS" IN CHURCH

My introduction to this colourful and delightful institution, was in my early days as a member of Thaxted Church. I would go into church on the days when I knew Mrs. Noel would be there, busily arranging flowers for the following Sunday. It was a joy and an inspiration to watch her producing beautiful pictures with flowers and foliage. It was my privilege to help by fetching water, to empty or fill vases, and sometimes to bring in flowers from my own garden, but not to arrange them! She had a wonderful sense of colour and would produce marvellous effects in glowing and eye-catching colours.

The Church is so large and spacious, that it needs good masses of colour, bright orange, pure yellow and all shades of red. This she achieved with old-fashioned country garden flowers in good solid earthenware jugs and pots, placed on the floor, and always looking as though they were still growing out of the earth. No pedestals with hot-house blooms for "Mother Minno" as we called her. I learnt a great deal from watching her at work, to mass the colours and avoid spotty effects by putting in odd blooms dotted about. In those days every pot of flowers had its own position and its meaning; one by the Madonna and the crucifix, copper bowls on the alter railings, a vase for St Francis or St George, and one at the base of each banner and so on. The church was ablaze with lovely flower pictures, and each season had its own particular flower in a certain place. I remember at Easter the orange or yellow crown imperials in quaint glass bottles on the screen leading into the Becket Chapel. And Whitsun was the time when two very large pots filled with sheep's parsley, or Queen Anne's lace according to the flower arrangers, gathered from the churchyard by small boys, were placed in the chancel and looked just heavenly there in the sunlight from the beautiful windows in the Lady Chapel.

Years later when Mrs Putterill took her mother's place I was then able to help her "do" the flowers, together with other helpers who undertook the task of filling one or more vases. It was a great joy to be able to create lovely masses of colour for the big pots, or to find tiny exquisite blooms for the small vases or pottery rings which were placed in various niches.

It took many hours of one's time, first of all choosing and cutting the flowers and foliage, then arranging it all. But it was a very enjoyable task and the result was usually worth the trouble. Sometimes we had very few flowers and then again perhaps too many. I remember one occasion when we had spent a long time "doing" for the Harvest Festival. We were weary, thirsty and grubby, and taking a final satisfied look round, were making for the door, home and a rest, when in came two well-meaning people with a bath full of asters and short ones at that! What to do with them? I forget what we did do with them, but I know I have never cared much for asters since!

Dahlias too can be a problem; they are either too big, too floppy, too dark or too short-stalked. But they will turn up for the Harvest Festival, and must have their place among all the other flowers. One traditional decoration at this time was a beautiful sheaf of corn, which had been specially cut and tied, and also guarded from hungry mice in the barn! It was placed in the crossing under the Stella, and trimmed with a few lovely bright orange cape gooseberry pods.

For Christmas of course there were many Christmas trees to be carefully decorated, and the Crib to be trimmed with trailing ivy and greenery, and if possible a few Christmas roses or yellow winter jasmine in front of the figure of Mary.

Easter-tide brought out the Pascal Candle to be decorated with four small coloured glasses filled with a few dainty spring flowers, primroses, blue scillas, violets and daisies.

The niche in the North Porch also had its pot of flowers for any festival Sunday. That I liked to do and to make a good job of it too, as I can see that from my front windows; and unless it has some good strong colours in it, it just doesn't mean a thing. So in go the brightest of flowers, orange marigolds, red poppies, yellow doronicums, phlox or gay roses, to show up against the old grey stone and flint surround.

Sometimes, of course, one has had failures or "flops", and that reminds me of what might once have been a really good "flop". A rather tallish vase on the ledge of the pulpit had too many flowers in it and looked to be rather too heavy for safety. I remember looking at it on Sunday as I sat in my seat listening to the sermon wondering if it would stand up to the movement of the preacher. Supposing he got excited and waxed eloquent. What might happen to the vase, not forgetting the flowers and the water. In the line of danger sat three unsuspecting servers; who would get the vase on his head, who would have the flowers for a crown and which one would get the baptism of unholy water? I watched and waited, but luckily the sermon was quite a mild one, so the vase stayed up on its ledge and all were safe. Years later when the pulpit was being repaired, I suggested that a small shelf be placed in the back of the pulpit under the existing crucifix and that was well done and made a safe and lovely position for a good vase of flowers.

Owing to illness and other causes, I gave up this delightful occupation for some years, but later on I found myself taking

Photo by John Gay

on the job again of "doing the church flowers". With at first a few helpers but soon these faded away and I was left to carry on solo. This I did for some time until I broke my left wrist and found I could not even cut the flowers from my garden. But a good friend, Dolly, came to my rescue and between us we carried on the good work. Later I persuaded another friend, Dora, to help and for several years we three got together every Friday morning and made many lovely arrangements of flowers gathered from our own gardens, or brought in sometimes by one or two interested church members. Often, we felt that no-one noticed or appreciated our efforts and at times it was difficult to get enough flowers. Perhaps Stanley had forgotten to unlock the back door, so we couldn't get to the water tap and the dustbin and our own back-aches were not helpful, for we had no table to work on and the floor seemed a long way down. So at last we decided we had done our bit and would retire gracefully, leaving the job for someone else.

---

*One day when Kate was flower arranging in the church and these two American ladies came in with several children and they went and started to do brass rubbings in the chancel, and they put their papers all out and they got on with it and these children were running about, tearing round, making a noise and jumping all over the place in the church. Well Kate had had enough and so she went up to them and said "Now look here, keep those children quiet." she said, "We don't want all that noise in here, this is a church." And one of the American ladies, she said, "I don't suppose the Lord would mind." "No, perhaps not," said Kate,* **"but Father Jack Putterill would!**

This happened one day when I was chatting away to Kate about various things, mainly to do with her work, her weaving and a collage she was doing. She was then about one hundred and two or three. Then we lapsed into a silence and then she suddenly said, "I wonder how the Archbishop's getting on"? I thought, the Archbishop, how extraordinary, she said "Er, yes, I think he is in a bit of a difficult position". Then I suddenly remembered, that morning, during the "Today" programme, there had been a report about troubles in northern Nigeria with various religious factions and that the Archbishop had gone over there and had to have been as tactful as he possibly could. It so happened that my daughter was over in Nigeria with her husband, where he was working and so we had been talking about her. It was extraordinary that she was still listening to the "Today" programme and taking notice of things like that and making connections. It was quite amazing that she had suddenly thought about the Archbishop.

# PART OF THE STORY OF CHURCH HOUSE, THAXTED, IN THE COUNTY OF ESSEX

We don't know all the story of this old house, but we feel it must have been an important one in Tudor times, late 15th. century. The main part of the building may have been erected as a dwelling place for masons and workers who were building or adding to the church. On one wall we found traces of wall paintings showing the white rose of York, Cecily of York, but alas! too faint to keep. The back part of the building was probably a cottage, one room up and one down, with very heavy rough beams and low ceiling, and a brick floor. This appears to have been linked on to the front building, and other rooms added at each side. There is no sign of a stairway anywhere, unless it was at the end of the "Tappy", as Lizzey White the last owner, called it. The room above the "Tappy", my bedroom, is smaller than this one, with a spare space large enough for a stairway. Part of this is now made into a cupboard while the rest is just an empty space we call it the "Priest's Hole".

There was a tiny bedroom just at the top of the front staircase, partitioned off and papered with dark blue wallpaper. Alone I knocked down this partition stripped off some of the paper and found beautiful beams, and what so obviously looked like the outside wall of the first building. This room we made into a "Sanctum" with a divan under the window and lots of cushions, and used it as a place to sit and listen to recordings, or to watch the weddings, as the window faced the North Door of the church, and gave a marvellous view of everything.

The big front room with lovely carved beams had the first treatment, and eventually made a very good shop with plenty of shelves and tables for displaying weaving, pottery, woodwork etc, etc. And after several months and years of hard work and patience we were rewarded for the result was very attractive and interesting. However, just as things were beginning to work out well, came 1939 and war. That meant, closing down and giving up weaving for some time. When at last came peace, we were able to pick up the pieces, or the shuttles, and get busy again.

Now the small shop next door, which had been let to A. Bishop, was vacant and ours to open up into the big shop. The outside door into the street was taken down, the walls re-plastered and it was now made into a workshop with two looms and benches for woodwork. We at last had the use of the big cellar under the main building, and a long north facing window looking out on to the garden. The "Tappy" could now be used as a sitting room, though it had an ugly fireplace a very uneven floor and horrible boarding round the lower half of the walls,

Church House, showing the shop next-door which was able to be reincorporated when it became vacant.

and all rather damp and smelly. But that was to be the last room to be restored. It had served its purpose as a weaving room for some time, warmed by an anthracite stove brought up from the Priory studio. Later I had a loom upstairs in the middle room, with a good little stove which could be kept going and so was most useful, and I could work up there in the evenings. I think we have had looms or spinning wheels busy in most parts of the old house. It has always been a workshop, given over to all kinds of handwork, with wool, wood, clay, painting, printing, puppetry etc.

The room I am sitting in now is part of the old cottage, and was the kitchen, with a brick floor that had a hollow in the middle, an extra door and only one small window, and of course a kitchen range. This was pulled out and a fireplace bricked in with hobs for logs, and many log fires have burned there in our time. We did have a very good fireback, but we burnt that out! At first we concreted the floor, having removed and kept the old bricks, but later we had a boarded floor put down. So with an extra window, a door removed, and

84

bookshelves in the corner it is now our favourite eating and sitting place, very cosy and quiet.

Our kitchen was at first very primitive, a pump over the stone sink, a very small window, and no means of cooking except for a gas ring and a tin oven! Now it has good cupboards and shelves, a long workbench, a solid fuel boiler to heat water and radiators in the bathroom next door, electric cooker and a 'fridge in the cupboard under the stairs. These fittings were designed for us by John Hunter, and made by Denis Andrews working for P. Francis. With pale green Formica tops and plain wooden doors with good knobs all really transformed the kitchen into a pleasant though oddly shaped room.

There were two stables built on to the old kitchen, one in a bad state of repair so it was pulled down and the other divided in two, one half to make a bathroom and the other to serve as a dye shed, fitted with hot and cold water, a sink, Calor gas and a copper for washing fleeces and dyeing hand spun wool for tweeds. This dye-shed opened on to a good open yard, very convenient for drying both fleeces and yarns. This at first was a muddle of cobbles, cinders and rough tufts of grass. But later we had it levelled and concreted to make a good patio, with a flower border along the wall and a bed of flowering shrubs facing south. This makes an ideal spot for sitting out in the sun, when we get some, and for tea in the garden.

When the cottage next door was sold to Mr. Latham, they took down the wooden lean-to kitchen with the horrible smoking chimney which for years had spoilt the outlook of our small

back sitting room. We then were able to move a small greenhouse which covered the windows of this room, its only use being to protect us from the filthy smoke from this kitchen chimney. With this removed and the garden planted, we now at last had a very much pleasanter view from these windows. How long it takes to get things put right and as one wants them to be. We had worked on and improved the interior of the house, but now the plastered front and one side were getting very weak and patches were falling off. At last we decided to get this done, and so in 1953 the work started. The old plaster was stripped off, and new laths and wire mesh made a good foundation for the new plaster. Sid Sutton, a very good plasterer, under-took the job, and we asked him to do pargetting with a pattern of twisted skeins of wool. We had some help from a friendly Suffolk builder, who unhappily could not get us the traditional comb for marking such as was used there, but by trial and error and experiments with table forks, a potato masher, and various garden tools a copper comb was made, and Sid practised his pattern. His mate shaped the panels, and the skeins had to fit in these. It was a tricky job and all to be done free-hand. As Sid began work on the morning after Coronation celebrations, he decided to begin on the side wall of the house rather than the front as his hand might not be too steady. It was a marvellous bit of work and looked lovely, and is still much admired. Before this we planned to have a large bow window in the shop front and another in the front workshop, so they were designed by Gerald Lacoste and put in before the plastering began. We also had new cedar gates for the yard entrance and now the front was complete and looked fine, and the big windows gave us so much more needed light indoors.

1966. The last room to be renovated was the "Tappy" which needed a new floor, ceiling beams to be uncovered and a good fireplace. Gradually this was achieved after much care and thought. The fireplace was built by Percy Baker, and was a great improvement though it lacks a good solid oak beam for a mantel. Many friends have promised to find a big beam but so far nothing has been forthcoming. There were traces on one wall of paintings of the white rose of York, but it was so faint that we felt it was useless to try and preserve them, so we took photographs instead. Gary Greenwood made some good oak shelves to fit in each side of the fireplace to hold books and recording sets and loud speakers, etc. So with the piano in the corner and various easy chairs of different ages, it is now our music room, and is a very pleasant place in both winter and summer.

# THE GARDEN AT CHURCH HOUSE THAXTED

When we bought this house in 1932, we were so overcome by its size and poor condition that we kept away from it for some days or weeks. The same applied to the garden, for it really was a wilderness, nasty evergreen shrubs, many self-seeded holly trees, sycamore saplings and three limes at the far end. There was a rickety summer house and various bits of brick walls in many stages of decay, poor paths and no flowers except a few yellow tulips and lots of wild white violets, and a white jasmine climbing up the barn. We still have that and the violets.

The fence between us and the cottage next door was very low so we gave them a few feet and put up a six-foot tin fence which we covered with wattle hurdles. Later we had the three limes pulled out, and a good high wall replacing the low one, using old bricks inside from the odd bits of wall in other parts of the garden.

Another eyesore was an enormous shed, used for garaging three cars at one time, and later storing rubbish, ours or other folks. This was replaced by a smaller brick one with good windows, and was to be a coal and wood shed. But I made it into a pottery studio, fitted with wheels, kiln, a long bench, and lots of shelves for the pots. It was a very pleasant place for working. Today, 1987, it is now our gardening shed.

At the same time we got Percy Baker to put down good brick paths round the garden beds, and some crazy paving near the greenhouse. These paths save a great deal of work as they

needed no weeding, and also mean that one can always walk round the garden even in the wettest of weather. There was a well in the garden from which came the water for that pump over the sink. So that was blocked up and a circular pool built over it. Our friend and nurseryman Arthur built a rockery with lovely Westmorland rocks on each side, and that made a very fine feature in the garden. Alas! it is now rather overgrown with twitch and bellbine as we find it difficult to get on it or off it to weed. But the pool is fine and is home for a good family of goldfish.

The plan of the garden was often altered until we had the brick paths, but now it remains fairly static. There are various flowering shrubs, and lots of good herbaceous plants, which fight a yearly battle with ground elder. There are a few roses even dating back to 1934 and every year we grow some annuals to fill in empty spaces. So there are nearly always some flowers to pick for the house or to give away to friends.

I once had a herb garden which included most common and some uncommon herbs, but some were such rank growers and very few had coloured flowers that I gave it up and used a small bed near the kitchen for the ones most needed for cooking. I concentrated on growing tall herbaceous plants to give me plenty of strong colourful flowers for use in "doing the flowers for church". It is interesting to note that every year we get plants of the wild mignonette or dyer's weed which we used to dye our yarn a beautiful yellow. I had a lovely coat of that colour.

We have tried sometimes to grow a few vegetables but found it not very practical except for runner beans, which are good to look at as well as to eat. In the early days we bought and planted several ornamental and flowering trees and some fruit trees as well, but they had to come out as they took up too much room. By trial and error a garden is made, and even after fifty odd years one can still see many mistakes in planning at least, but I usually have a brave show, if a trifle muddled.

---

*Kate loved her garden, she didn't want anyone else to do anything in it, she would be muddling about out there and I was in the house doing things. One day it came on to rain, so I said, "Come on Kate you can't be out there in this weather its starting to rain. "Look here," she said "I'm not made of sugar." She said, "I'll come in when I'm ready!" Which she did.*

Kate, when in her nineties, was advised to use a walking frame which she treated rather with disgust. She hung her bag on the front in which she used to put her gardening tools. One day when she was out in the garden, she unfortunately wrong footed herself and fell and broke her hip.

She was taken into Addenbrookes and again unfortunately she did not have her hearing aids in. They were asking her questions and she was giving them the answers to the questions she thought they had asked. This caused, shall we say, some confusion! They arranged for her to be assessed by which time her hearing aids had caught up with her. They were asking questions like, "Who is the monarch?" "Well, Queen Elizabeth the Second".

"Who is the Prime Minister?" "Well, Tony Blair." Then various other questions and she was beginning to get rather fed up, so she fixed them with a look and said, "Now look here, I was a teacher for forty years, I retired in 1959, and I have no intention of teaching anyone ever again so I suggest if you want to find out any more you look it up for yourself in a book!"

# LETTERS FROM AMERICA

**These are parts of letters from cousin Lilly whose father was Kate's brother William. See also "My Mother's Early Days"**

*My father said he made a banjo when he was 12 years old after seeing one on a wharf when they were down the river at sea front. The sailor playing it was from America. I am writing it up as he told it and will send it. He said he made the metal parts in his uncle's machine shop, which uncle was that? By name. He said the banjo played and he sold it for a pound when he left England. Later he sold banjo's in his store in Carthage and other musical instruments. All the rest of his life he played a banjo and very well. He talked about unloading wheat from Australia. We had over 100 new calves in March out here. Marilyn often came and helped.*

*Carol has just been here for a week from Kirksville, Missouri. We are making copies of your story so the cousins in Sand-point Idaho can have one or more. You saw Deloris. My sister Alice visited with the ones at Sand point who have a meat curing plant. She says they do very well. I must mail this today. I miss Ken*
*With love from us all,*
*Cousin Lilly*

*My Dad saw a banjo when he was 12. He was down at the sea port with the tow boat. He couldn't find one to buy in England so*

92

he made one. It played too he said. When he came over here he sold it for a pound and used the money to come over. I'm writing this up and will typewrite it for you. He boiled the wood for 48 hours in his mother's kitchen to make it bend round. If he made others he did not say.

He played a banjo all his life here and bought and sold them in the store.

As my father grew older he sometimes rode the horse that pulled the boat up and down the river. This day the barge was tied up to the bank, so he sat in a chair on deck and played the concertina.

He was around 10 he said. It was Sunday, so he played hymns. A small church was not far off and it was near church time. Some of the church members were walking to the church and following the tow-path. As they passed the boat they began to stop and listen. Soon half a dozen had stopped to hear this small boy play. Church time came and was passing. When the minister came to the door, and began to scold my father for distracting his church members. So he quit playing and the church members went into church.

He told this to me once. I think it bothered him - and he probably got scolded too at home later.

We had flowers among the vegetables. Violas volunteer in the garden and Hollyhocks. We had Marygolds (sic) among the tomatoes, Canterbury Bell and Impatience in rubber tires of a car beside the house and ferns and others. Goldenrod in a damp low place below the apple orchard and wild flowers. Fragrant wild roses in June and a bed of tame ones by the garden, big pink ones.

Everyone is busy, Marilyn's youngest girl is starting college. Brookings South Dakota has about 7-8,000 students. Some from Iran and such countries. It is an agricultural College and Engineering.

Brad is busy feeding cattle in the pasture alternating prairie hay with alfalfa and he raises hogs too, and has two sows with baby pigs right now.

I am putting together a story or article for you which Marilyn will type for you as it will have around 500 words. He was playing a concertina when he left England and brought it with him and out to the Dakota County. He made and played a banjo in England but sold it there. Here he sold musical instruments in his store and was expert at playing a banjo. This is what I'm writing about. Two things he learned in England and expanded here.

I hope your weather is better and that you are keeping well. You and I. So many things I should know and there is no-one to to ask.

Love Cousin Lilly

Every town in South Dakota has a number. Wenida is 57578 But each state is numbered differently

# FROM A TRIBUTE GIVEN BY SYBIL COLLINGS - 17TH MARCH 2003

*One cannot speak of Kate without mentioning Arthur Caton. Her companion for over sixty years, who taught her to dye, spin and weave in her early days as a teacher. Together they shared many interests, all enjoyed in the marvellous and unique setting of Church House. In the early days, life was not easy for them. She would come home from school and take on her "other" work, including renovating and plastering but they enjoyed their life and took every opportunity to learn new skills and face new experiences. In school holidays, Kate travelled to various European countries, bringing back books and artefacts related to the arts and crafts of those countries.*

*Both Kate and Arthur had many acquaintances in Thaxted and from faraway places. She counted among her friends, Gustav Holst, known to them as "Gussie"; The well-known photographer, Johnnie Gay; Cedric Arnold; the weaver Charlie Williams; Edward Bawden; Dorothy Mahoney; Bernard Leach; Julian Bream and through the connection with Imogen Holst, they met Ben Britten, Ben Crosier and Peter Pears and many, many others. It is a tribute to Kate that many of her pupils from school are here today, and still remember the useful lessons in sewing and knitting.*

*Kate was never afraid to speak her mind, but she was not without a sense of humour and had the gift of being able to laugh at herself. How can we forget the many little stories which made us smile even after several re-tellings?*

# KATE THE FILM STAR!

Thaxted and many inhabitants were used by Lewis Gilbert when filming the location scenes in "Time Gentlemen Please" in 1952. Kate was one of the extras. In this scene Kate is seated at her loom

in her home. Also in the shot are Marjorie Rhodes and Sid James.

Towards the end of the film after an election for the Parish Council, there are wild scenes of country dancing by many locals. Kate is the musician and can just be seen playing her accordion under the Guildhall. Just as the dancing finishes she can be seen first playing the last few notes, then stepping back and closing her box. As this was a night-time scene she was paid twice as much, the grand sum of 2 guineas! However, she is not in the close-up scene which was filmed in a the studio with a different actress.

96

# KATE MAKES BRITISH PATHE NEWS

In 1961 Kate was filmed by British Pathe News for an item called "Village Observatory 1961". This was included in one of their newsreels.

If you would like to see more then go to https://www.britishpathe.com/video/village-observatory/query/Thaxted. It shows Town Street with almost as many parked cars as today and the Guildhall before the 1975 restoration work.

For copyright reasons I am not able to include a screen shot.

The photo below of Kate carding in her garden is just as good as any in the film!

> *I knew Kate from being at Primary School. She taught the top class and was a good teacher and she taught me to play the recorder.*

# LAMENT FOR THE DEPARTED

*Paint and paste in sad confusion;*
*We are under no delusion;*
*Music silent, bamboo scattered,*
*Piano most rudely shattered.*

*Hark the groans that J. 4. Utters,*
*Hear the Head who feebly stutters*
*As he strives to carry on*
*In the steps where She has gone.*

*How we miss you, dearest Kate,*
*School is in a sorry state.*
*Leave your pots and weeds and knitting*
*Come back quick for the First Sitting.*

*From the collection of kind words written when Kate retired from Thaxted School.*

---

**Cover Design by Lisa Zador**

The choice of the cover design came about due to a mis-understanding. Kate was interested in a technique for producing marbled paper designs developed by Sydney Cockerell, called "Cockerell Papers". Being told she was interested in cockerels, I assumed her interest was in the birds! So I searched for a design containing cockerels! Once chosen I decided it was too good not to use. See more of Lisa's designs at www.curiousprintandpattern.com

Editor